FIRST 50 FUN CHILDREN'S SONGS
YOU SHOULD PLAY ON THE PIANO

ISBN 978-1-70511-067-6

Visit Hal Leonard Online at
www.halleonard.com

Contact us:
Hal Leonard
7777 West Bluemound Road
Milwaukee, WI 53213
Email: info@halleonard.com

In Europe, contact:
Hal Leonard Europe Limited
42 Wigmore Street
Marylebone, London, W1U 2RN
Email: info@halleonardeurope.com

In Australia, contact:
Hal Leonard Australia Pty. Ltd.
4 Lentara Court
Cheltenham, Victoria, 3192 Australia
Email: info@halleonard.com.au

CONTENTS

ABC

Words and Music by ALPHONSO MIZELL,
FREDERICK PERREN, DEKE RICHARDS
and BERRY GORDY

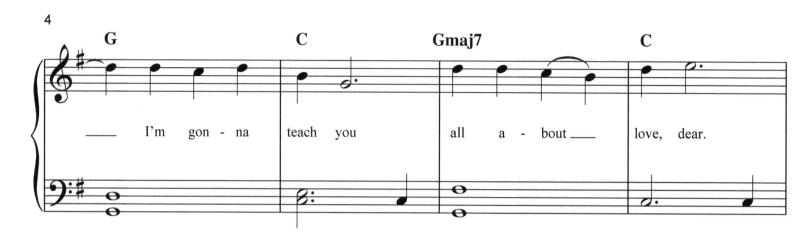

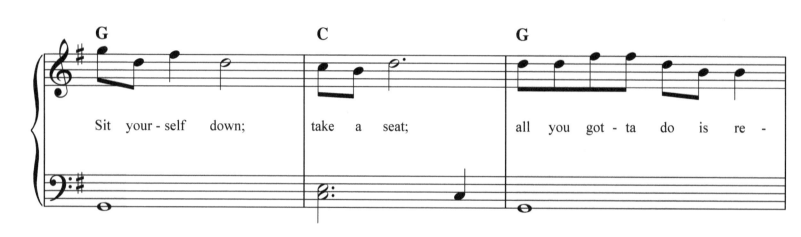

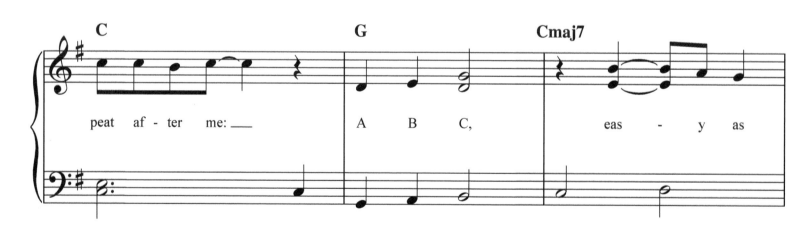

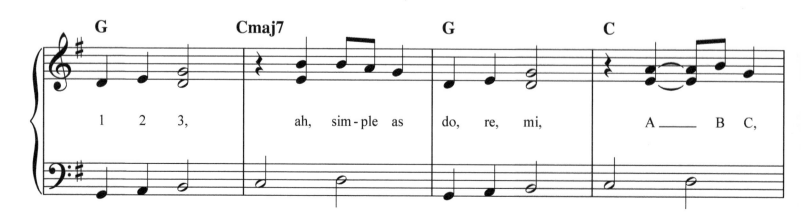

5

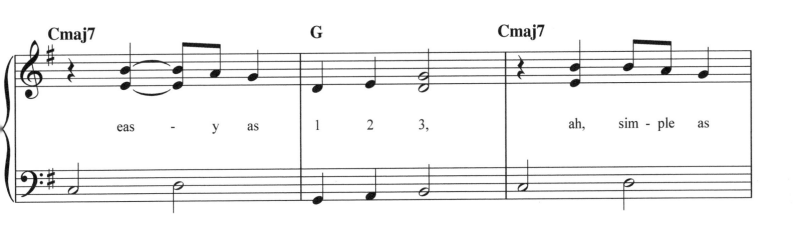

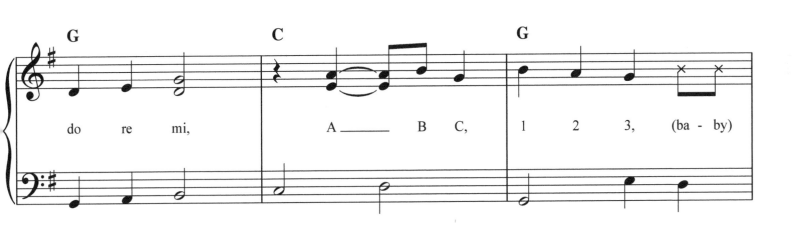

THE ANTS GO MARCHING

Traditional

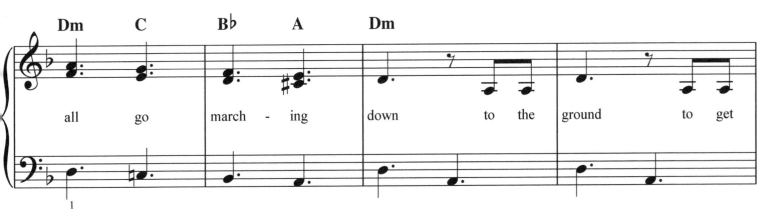

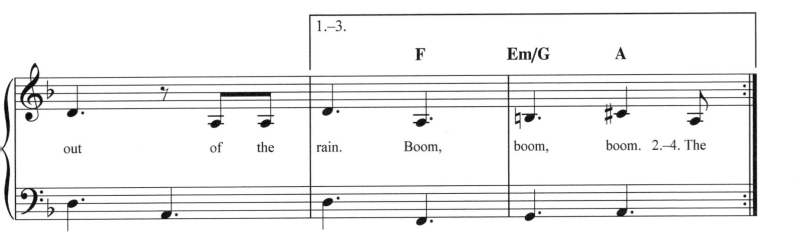

Additional Lyrics

3. The ants go marching seven by seven, hurrah! Hurrah!
   The ants go marching eight by eight, hurrah! Hurrah!
   The ants go marching nine by nine.
   The little one stops to check the time
   And they all go marching down to the ground
   To get out of the rain. Boom, boom, boom.

4. The ants go marching ten by ten, hurrah! Hurrah!
   The ants go marching ten by ten, hurrah! Hurrah!
   The ants go marching ten by ten.
   The little one stops to say "The end!"
   And they all go marching down to the ground
   To get out of the rain. Boom, boom, boom, boom!

BABY SHARK

Traditional Nursery Rhyme
Arranged by Pinkfong and KidzCastle

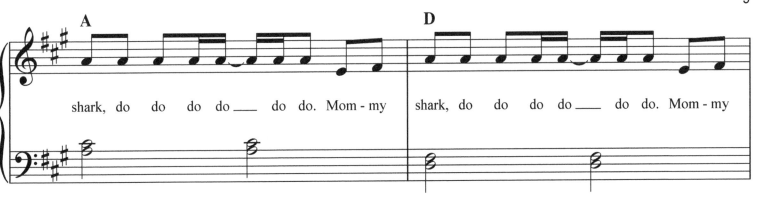

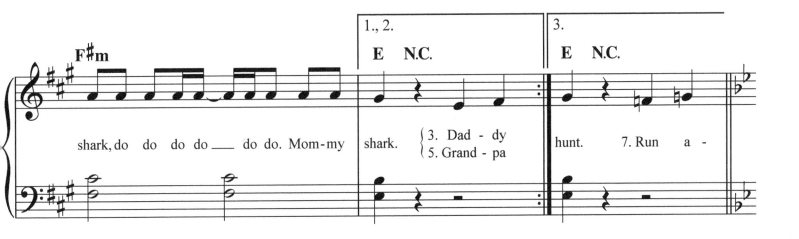

Additional Lyrics

3. Daddy shark, do do do do do do.
   Daddy shark, do do do do do do.
   Daddy shark, do do do do do do.
   Daddy shark.

4. Grandma shark, do do do do do do.
   Grandma shark, do do do do do do.
   Grandma shark, do do do do do do.
   Grandma shark.

5. Grandpa shark, do do do do do do.
   Grandpa shark, do do do do do do.
   Grandpa shark, do do do do do do.
   Grandpa shark.

6. Let's go hunt, do do do do do do.
   Let's go hunt, do do do do do do.
   Let's go hunt, do do do do do do.
   Let's go hunt.

THE BEAR WENT OVER
THE MOUNTAIN

Traditional

BE KIND TO YOUR WEB-FOOTED FRIENDS

Traditional

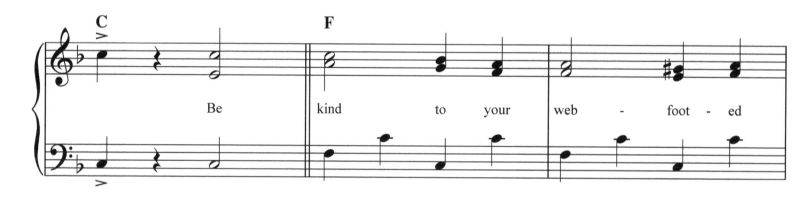

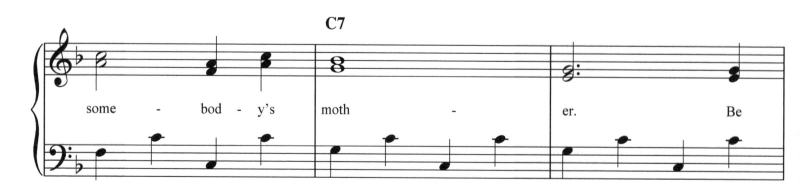

kind   to   your   friends   in   the   swamp _____

F   **Bb**

_____   where   it's   ver - y,   ver - y,   ver - y,   ver - y

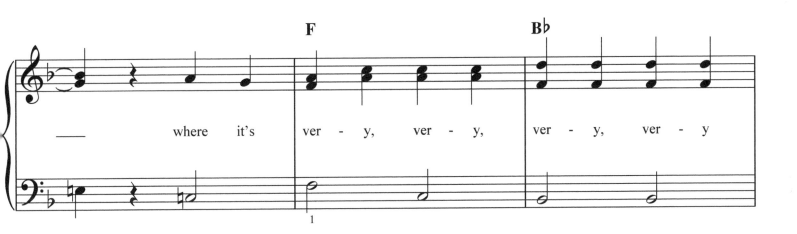

C   **F**

damp.   Now   you   may   think   that

this   is   the   end,   well,   it   is.

BINGO

Traditional

Moderately, with a lift

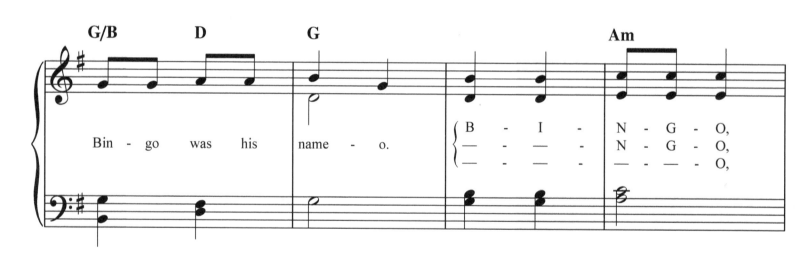

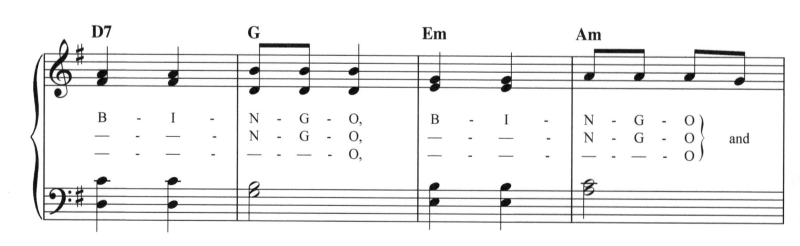

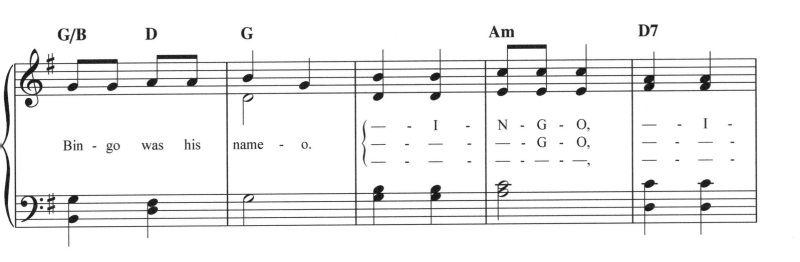

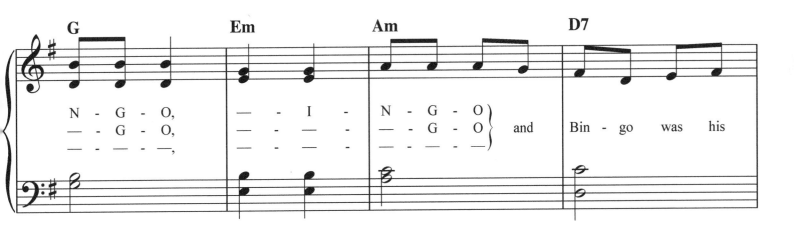

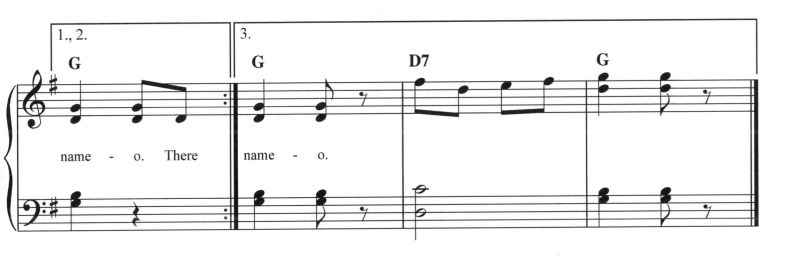

BLOWIN' IN THE WIND

Words and Music by
BOB DYLAN

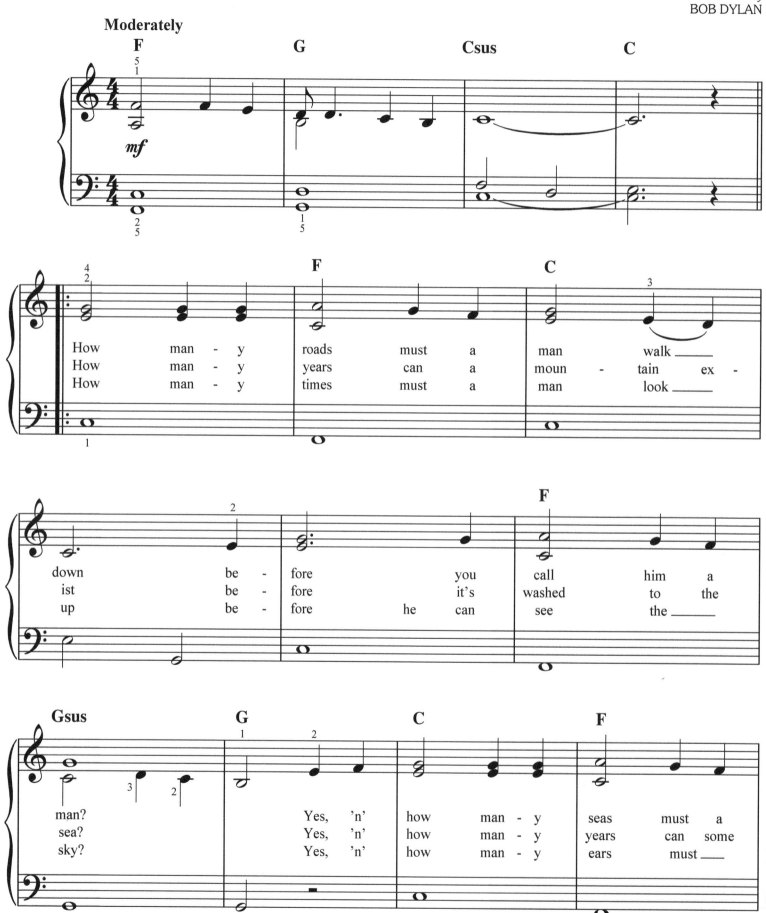

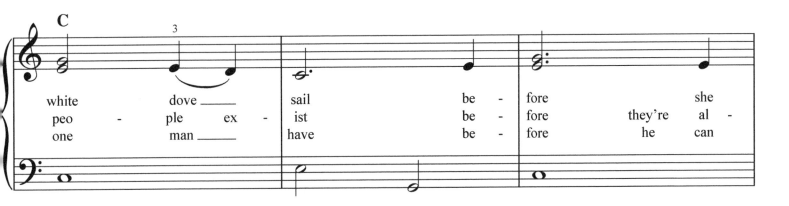

white dove ____ sail be - fore she
peo - ple ex - ist be - fore they're al -
one man ____ have be - fore he can

sleeps in the sand? ____ Yes, 'n' how man - y
lowed to be free? ____ Yes, 'n' how man - y
hear peo - ple cry? ____ Yes, 'n' how man - y

times must the can - non - balls ____ fly be -
times can a man ____ turn his head pre -
deaths will it take ____ till he knows that

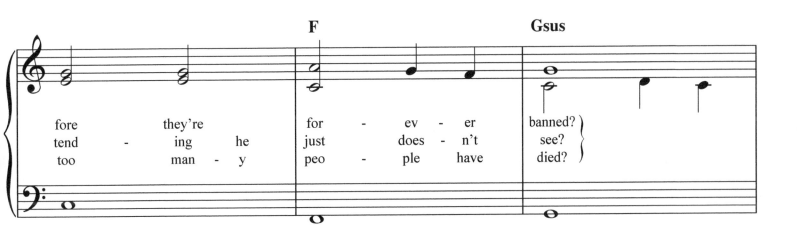

fore they're for - ev - er banned?)
tend - ing he just does - n't see?
too man - y peo - ple have died?

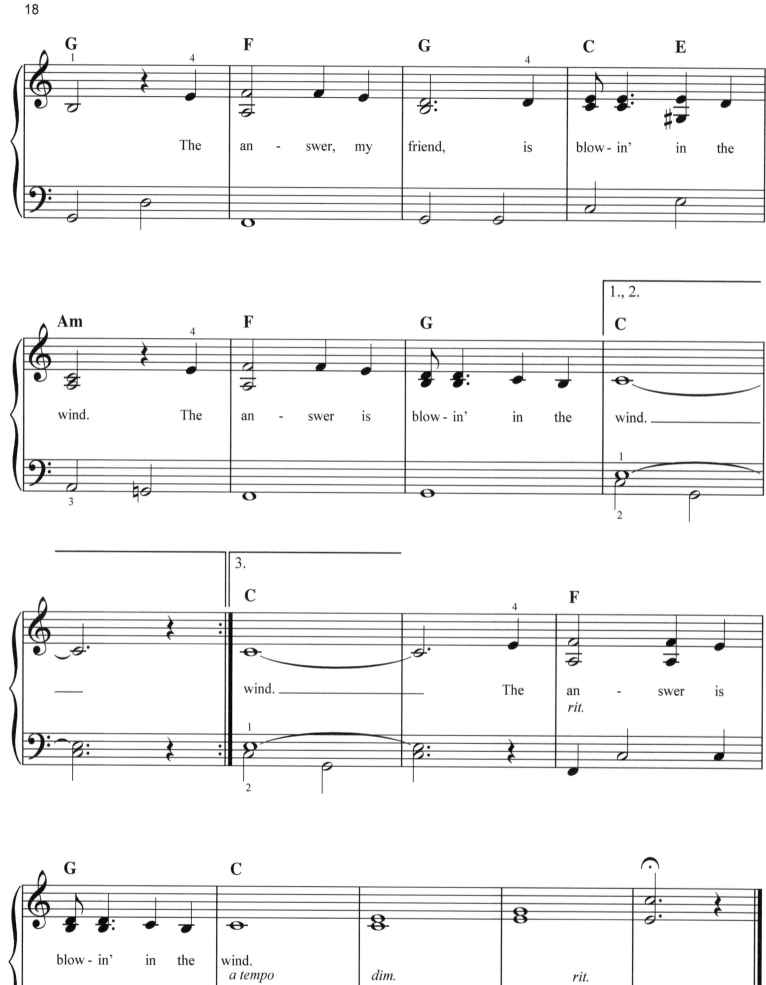

CASPER THE FRIENDLY GHOST

from the Paramount Cartoon

Words by MACK DAVID
Music by JERRY LIVINGSTON

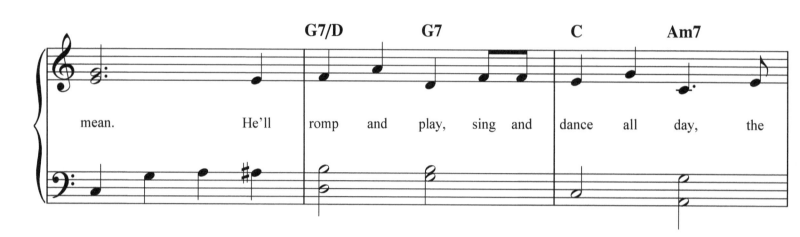

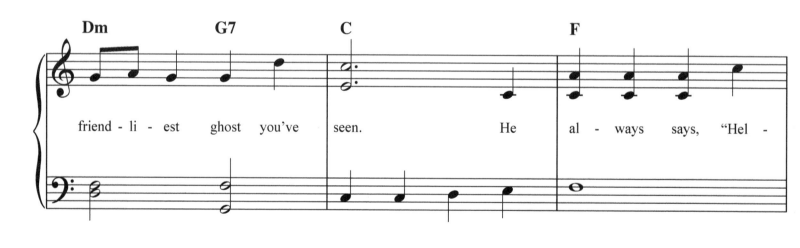

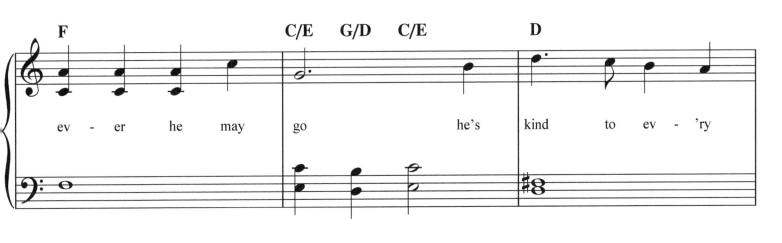

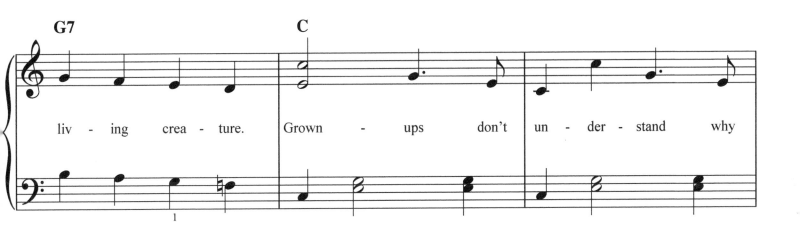

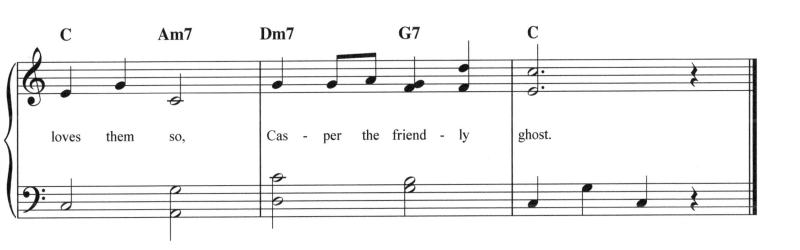

CANDLE ON THE WATER

from PETE'S DRAGON

Words and Music by AL KASHA
and JOEL HIRSCHHORN

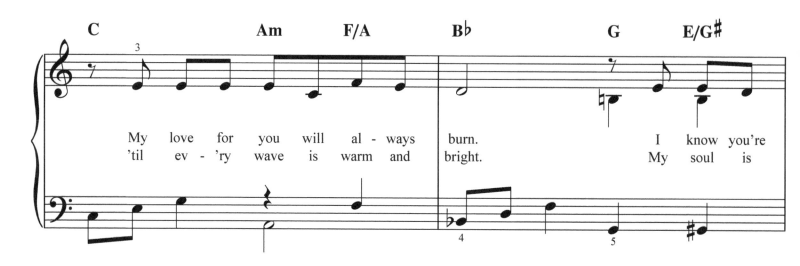

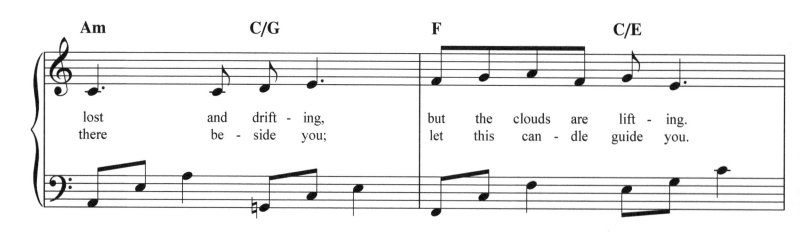

23

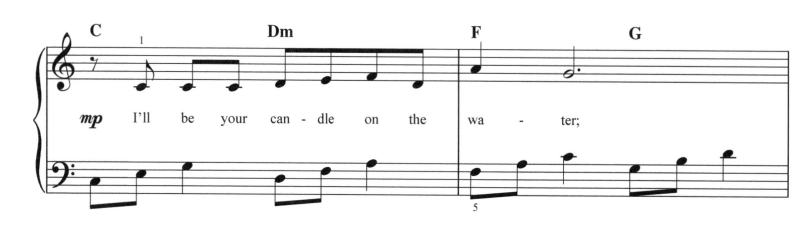

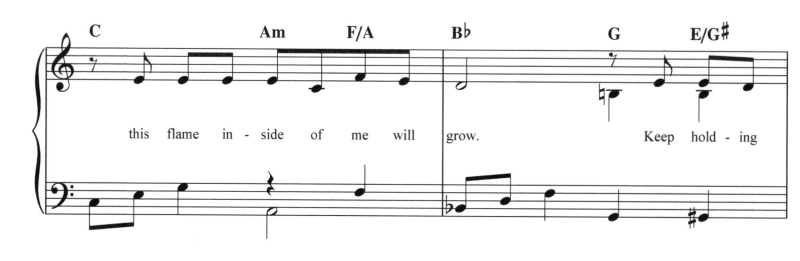

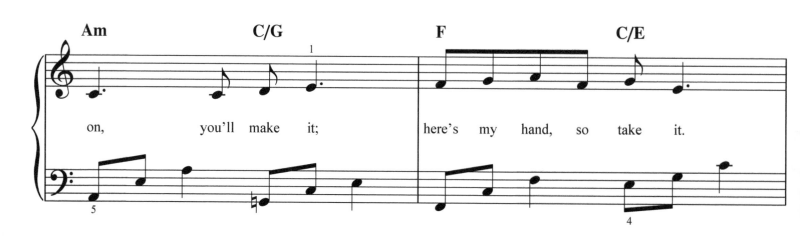

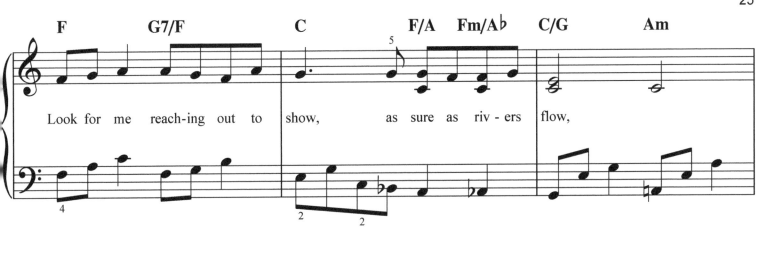

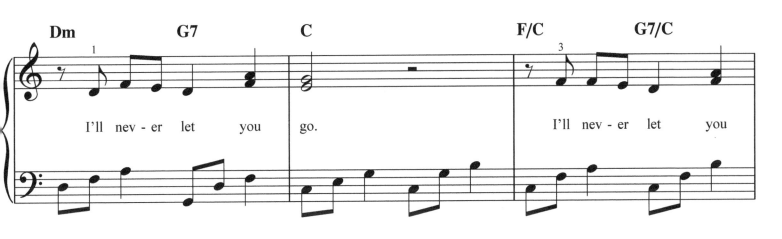

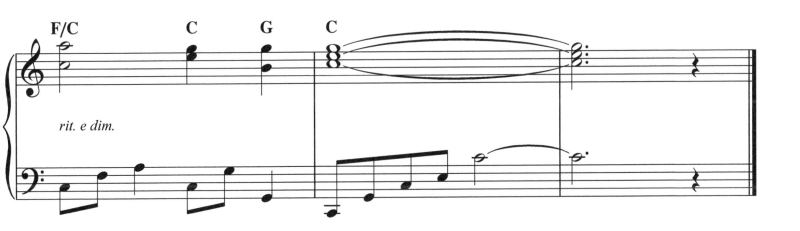

CRAZY LITTLE THING CALLED LOVE

Words and Music by
FREDDIE MERCURY

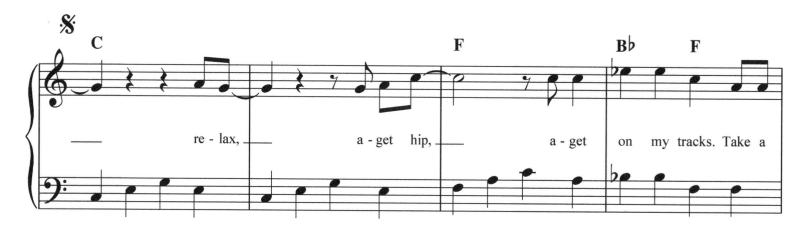

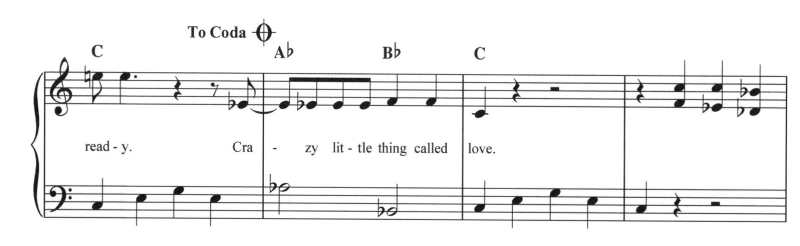

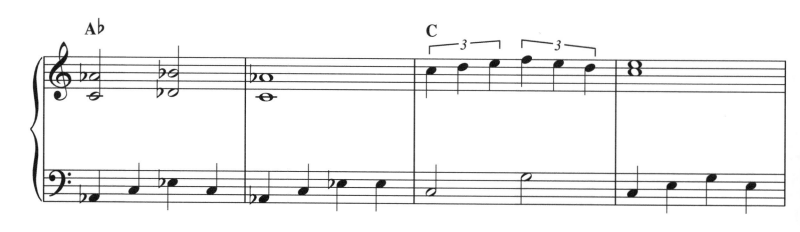

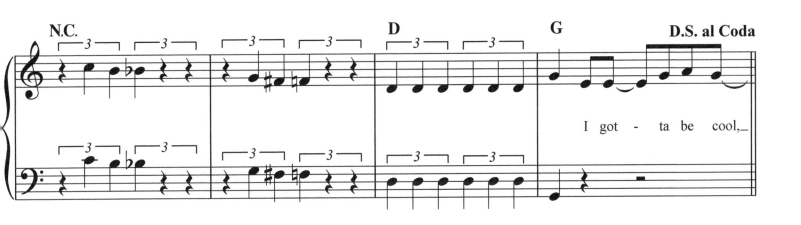

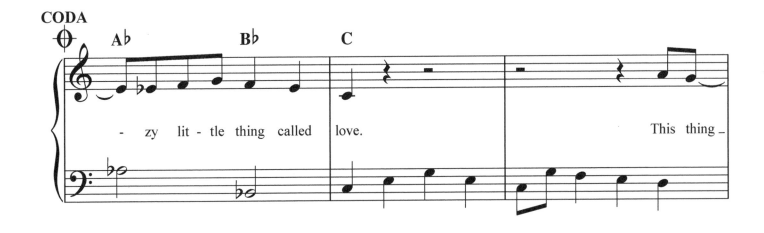

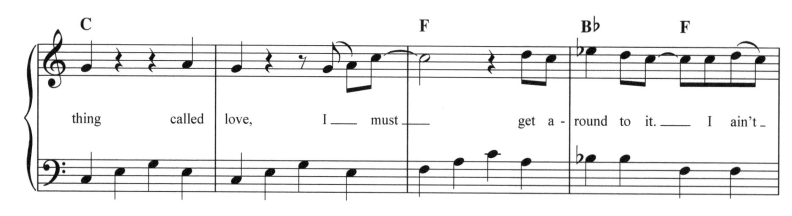

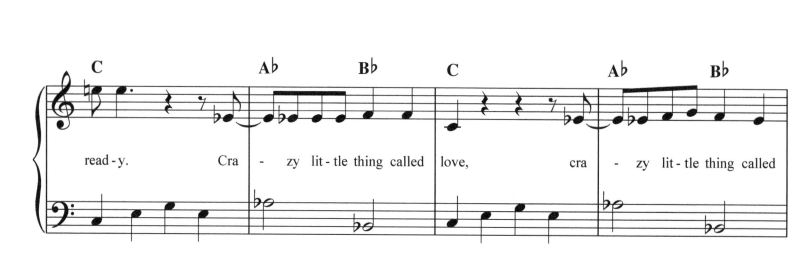

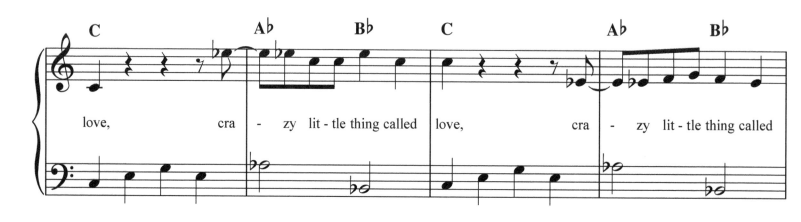

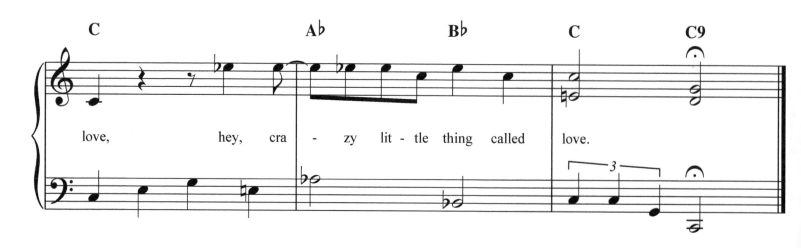

DOWN BY THE STATION

Traditional

CRUELLA DE VIL
from 101 DALMATIANS

Words and Music by
MEL LEVEN

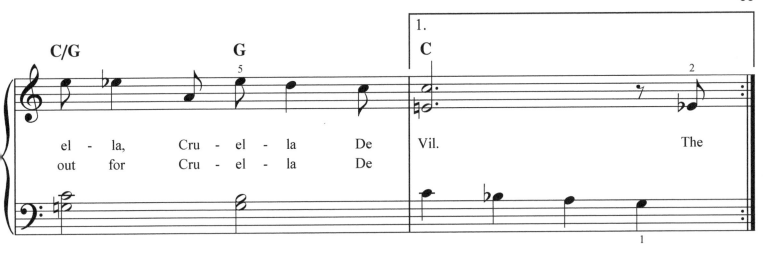

el - la, Cru - el - la De Vil. The
out for Cru - el - la De

Vil. At first, you think Cru - el - la is a dev - il, but

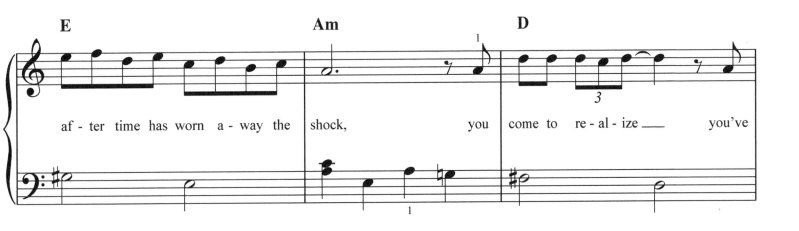

af - ter time has worn a - way the shock, you come to re - al - ize ___ you've

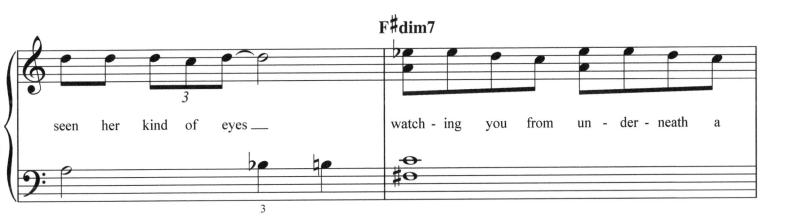

seen her kind of eyes ___ watch - ing you from un - der - neath a

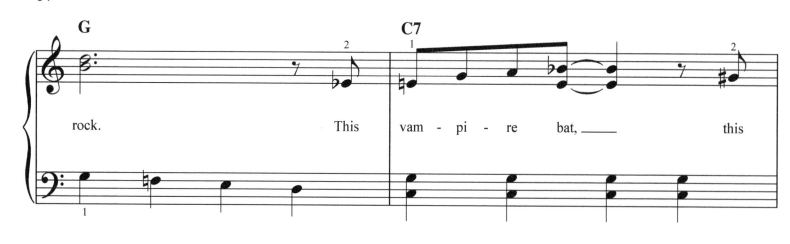

rock.   This   vam - pi - re   bat, _____   this

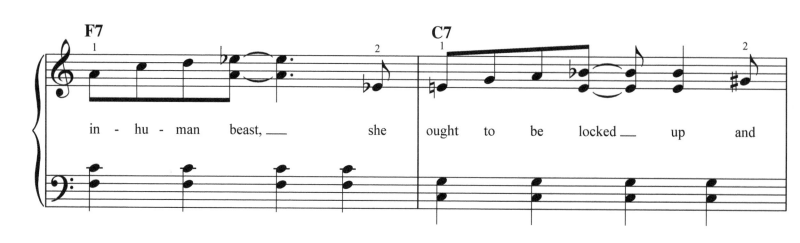

in - hu - man   beast, ___   she   ought   to   be   locked ___ up   and

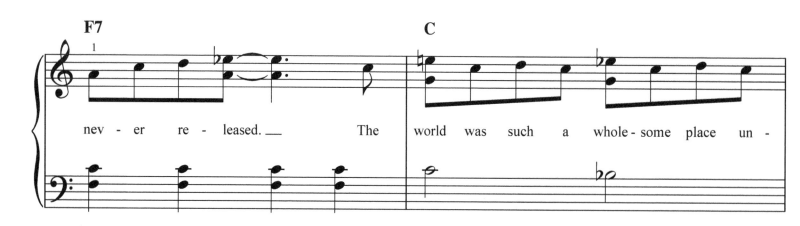

nev - er   re - leased. ___   The   world   was   such   a   whole - some   place   un -

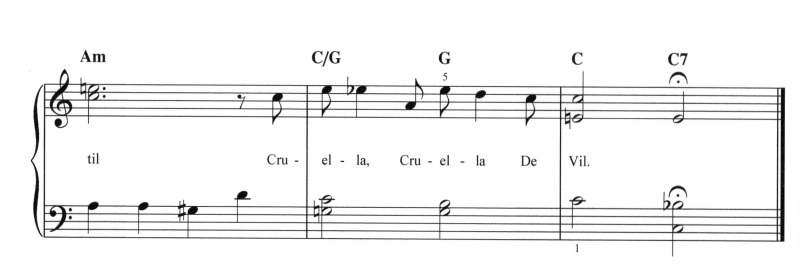

til   Cru - el - la,   Cru - el - la   De   Vil.

EVERYTHING IS AWESOME
(Awesome Remix!!!)
from THE LEGO MOVIE

Words by SHAWN PATTERSON
Music by ANDREW SAMBERG,
JORMA TACCONE, AKIVA SCHAFFER,
JOSHUA BARTHOLOMEW, LISA HARRITON
and SHAWN PATTERSON

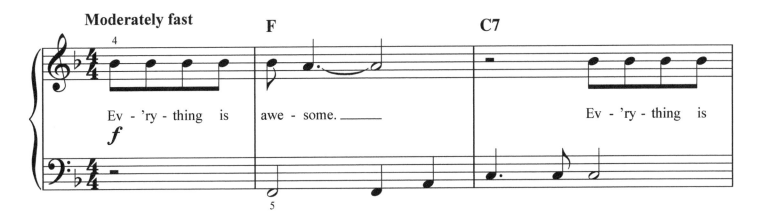

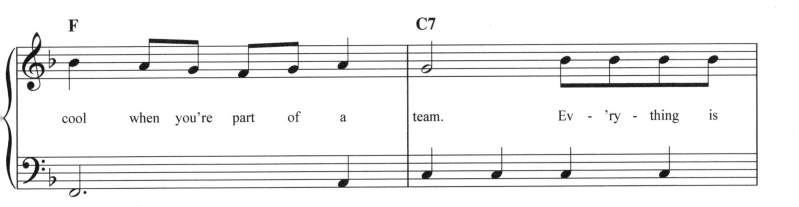

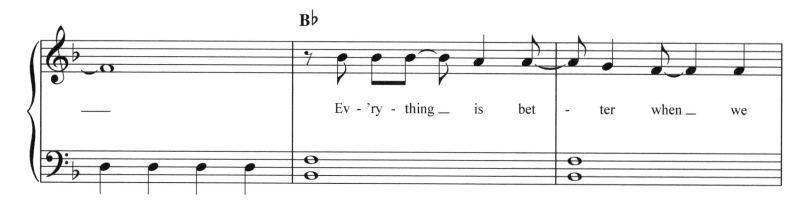

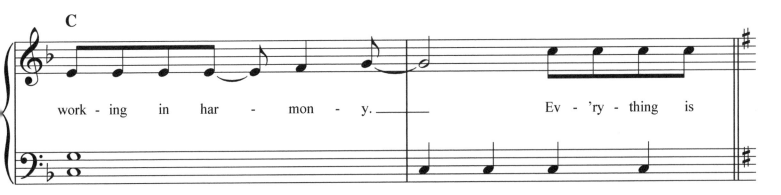

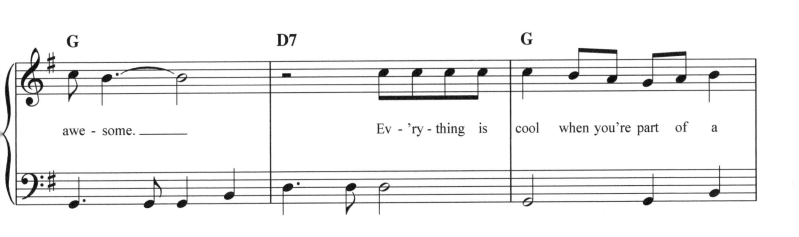

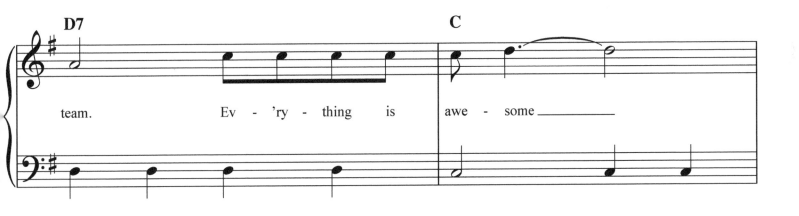

DOWN BY THE RIVERSIDE

African-American Spiritual

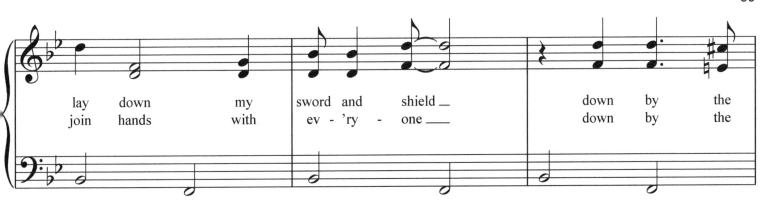

lay down my sword and shield ___ down by the
join hands my with ev - 'ry - one ___ down by the

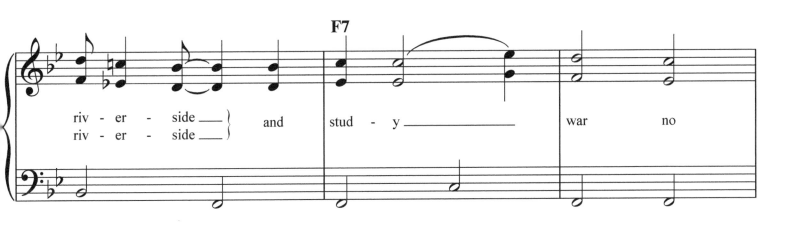

riv - er - side ___ and stud - y ___ war no
riv - er - side ___

1.
2.

more. Gon - na I ain't gon - na

stud - y war no more, ___ I ain't gon - na stud - y war no more, ___

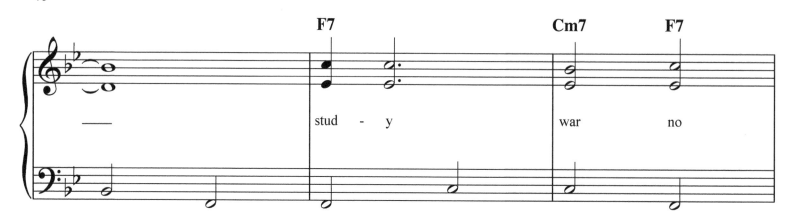

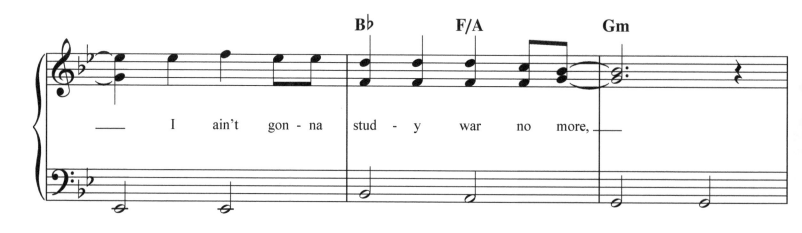

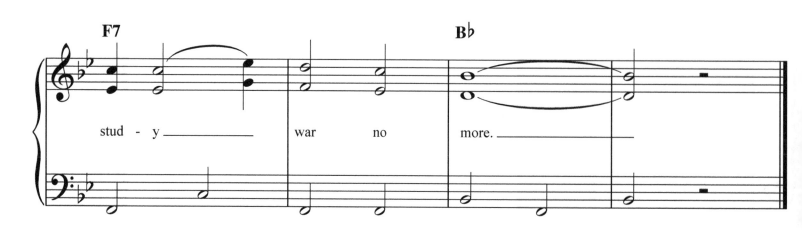

HEAD, SHOULDERS, KNEES AND TOES

Traditional

GIVE A LITTLE BIT

Words and Music by RICK DAVIES
and ROGER HODGSON

Moderate Rock

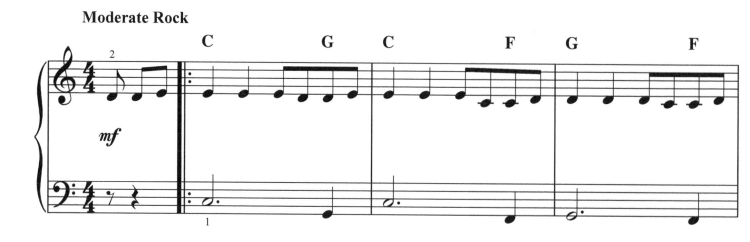

Give a lit - tle bit, _____

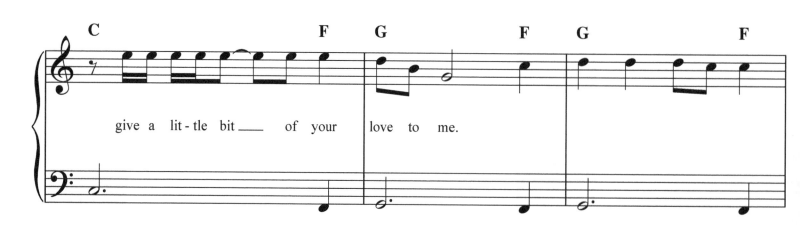

give a lit - tle bit ___ of your love to me.

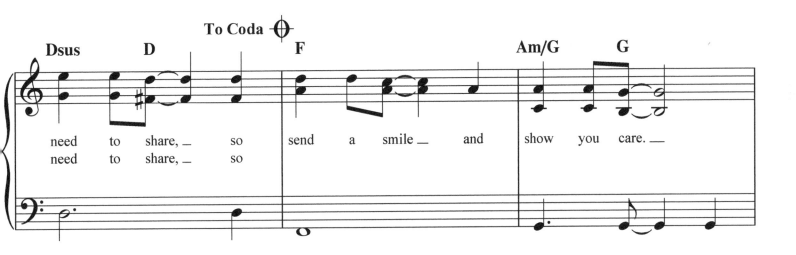

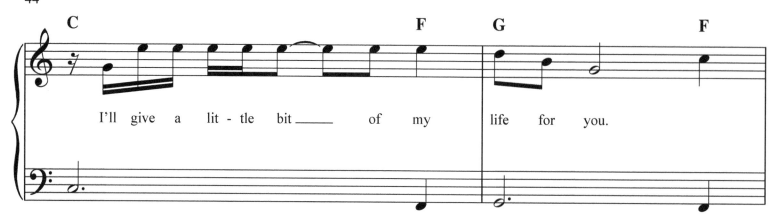

I'll give a lit-tle bit ____ of my life for you.

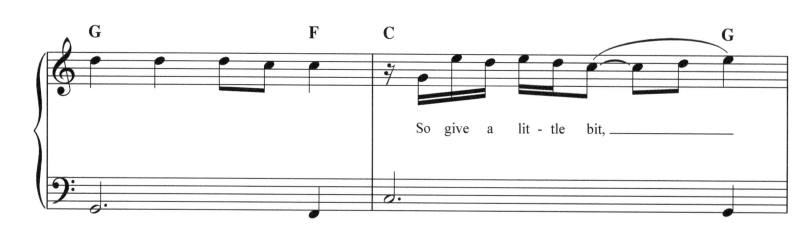

So give a lit - tle bit, _____

oh, give a lit-tle bit ___ of your time to me.

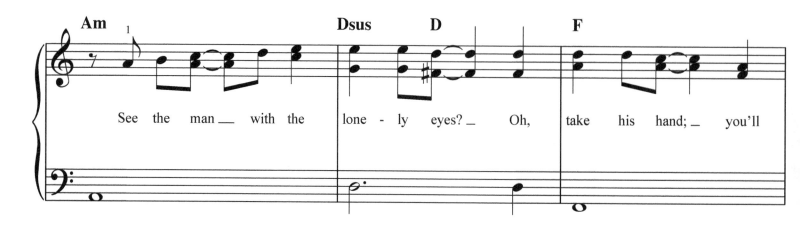

See the man ___ with the lone-ly eyes? ___ Oh, take his hand; ___ you'll

find your - self; _____ we're on our way _____ back

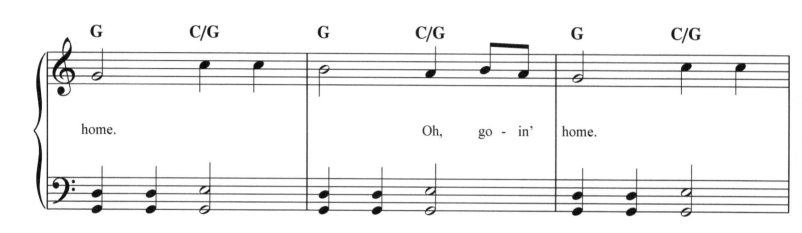

home. Oh, go - in' home.

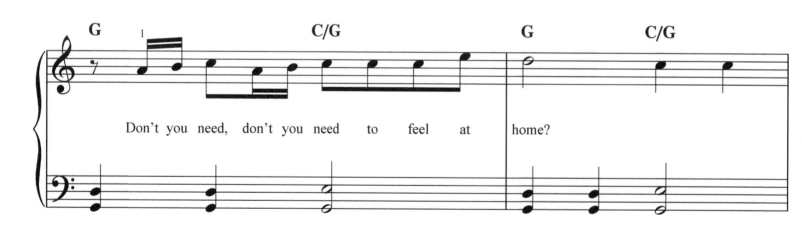

Don't you need, don't you need to feel at home?

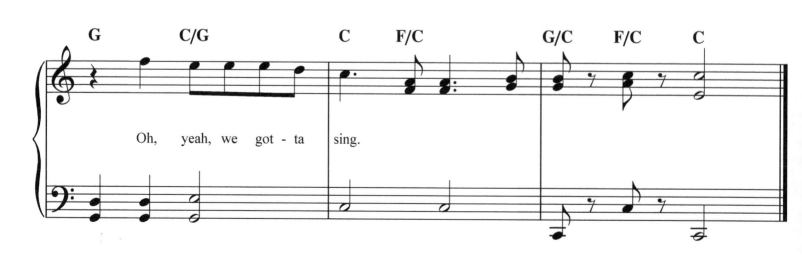

Oh, yeah, we got - ta sing.

HOW FAR I'LL GO

from MOANA

Music and Lyrics by
LIN-MANUEL MIRANDA

I've been ___ star - ing at the edge of the wa - ter ___ long ___ as I can re-

mem - ber, ___ nev - er real - ly know-ing why. I wish ___ I could be the per-fect

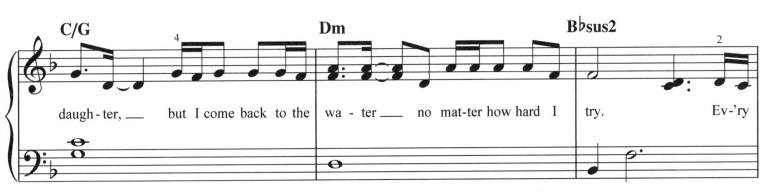

daugh - ter, ___ but I come back to the wa - ter ___ no mat-ter how hard I try. Ev-'ry

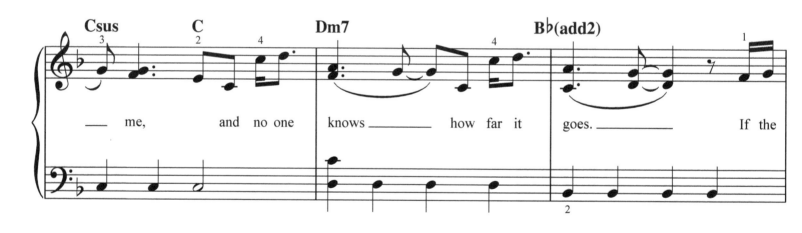

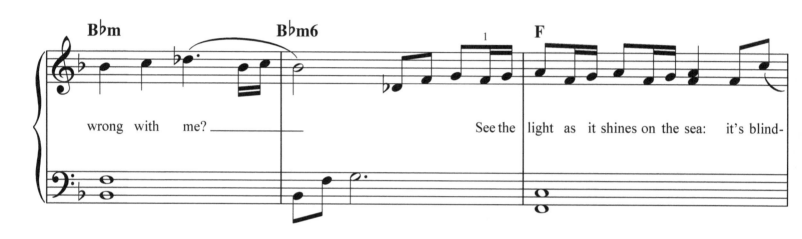

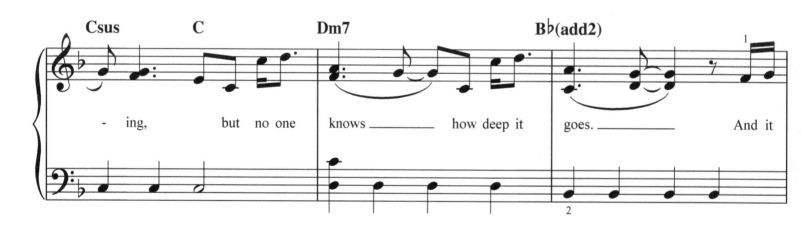

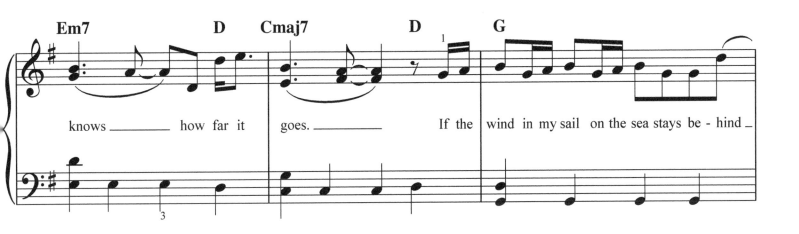

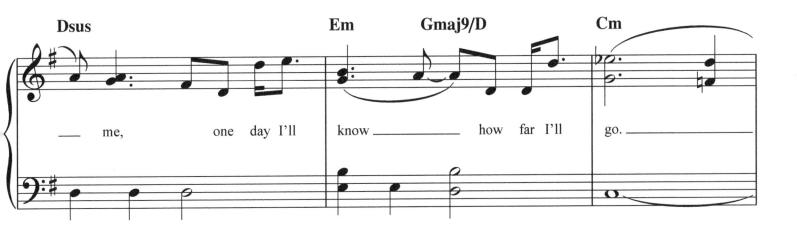

THE HAIRBRUSH SONG

Words by MIKE NAWROCKI
Music by MIKE NAWROCKI,
LISA VISCHER and KURT HEINECKE

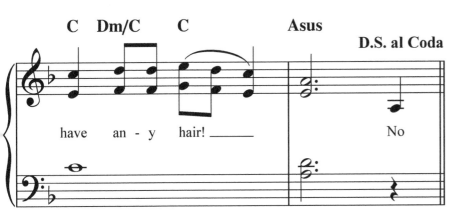

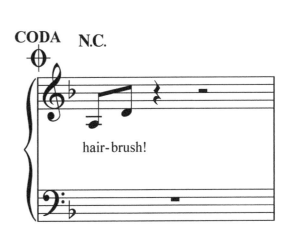

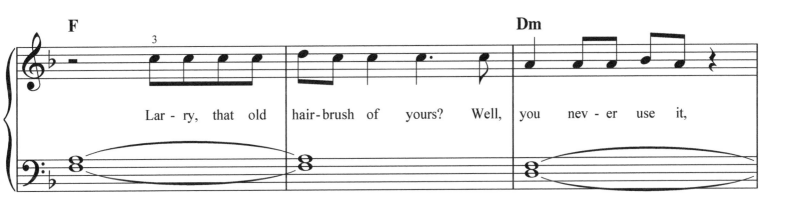

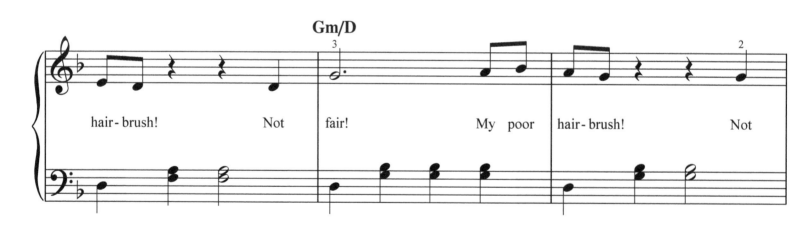

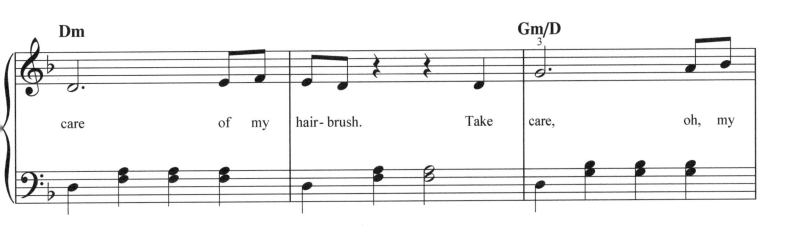

HAPPY
from DESPICABLE ME 2

Words and Music by
PHARRELL WILLIAMS

Moderately fast

It might seem
Here come bad

cra - zy what I'm 'bout to say.
news, _ talk - in' this and that.

Sun - shine, _ she's here; you can take a break.
Gim - me all you got, no _____ hold - ing back.

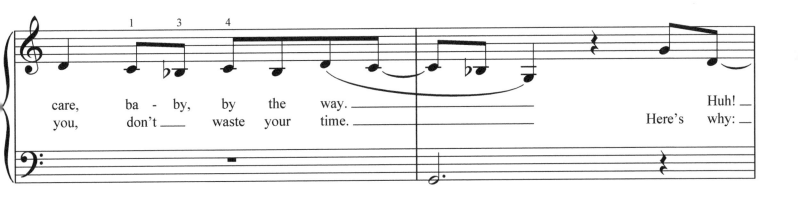

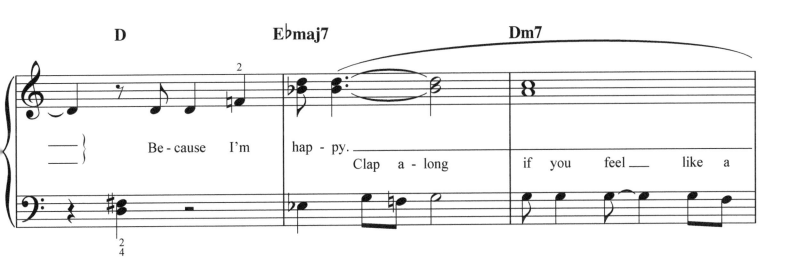

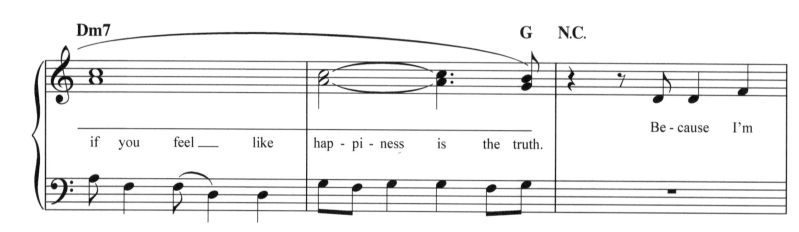

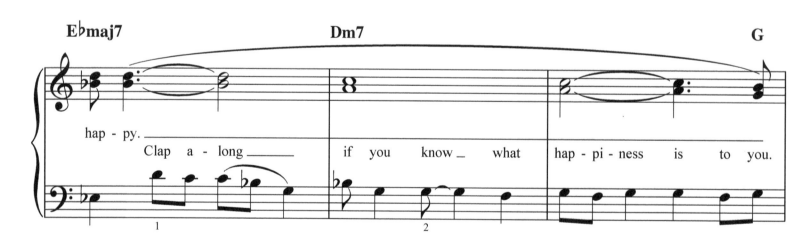

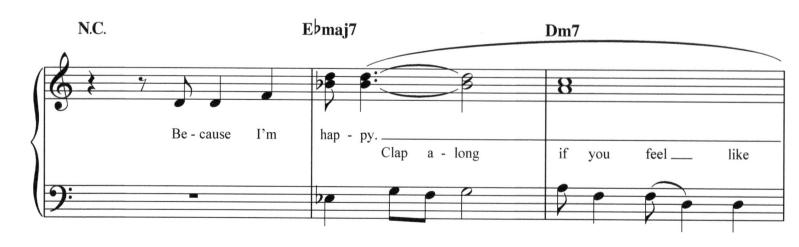

that's what you wan - na do.

Bring me down, __

__ can't noth - in'

bring me down; __

your love is too

high. Bring me down, __

can't noth - in'

bring me down. _

__ (Let me tell you now.)

Bring me down, __

can't noth - in'

bring me down; ___ your love is too high. Bring me down, __

___ can't noth - in' bring me down. ___ Be - cause I'm

E♭maj7　　　　　　　**Dm7**　　　　　　　**G**

hap - py. ___

Clap a - long if you feel ___ like a room with - out a roof.

4

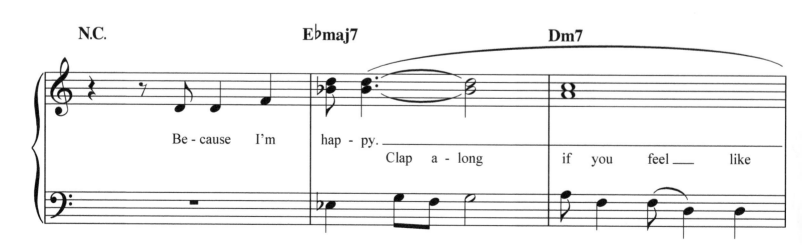

N.C.　　　　　　　**E♭maj7**　　　　　　　**Dm7**

Be - cause I'm hap - py. ___

Clap a - long if you feel ___ like

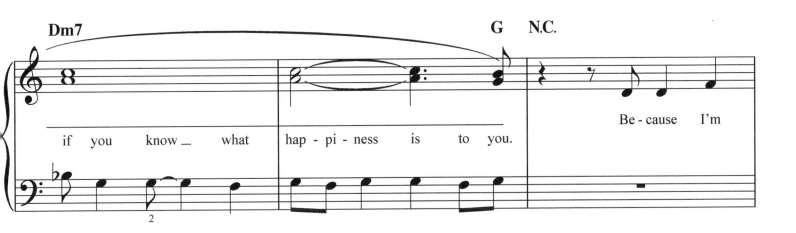

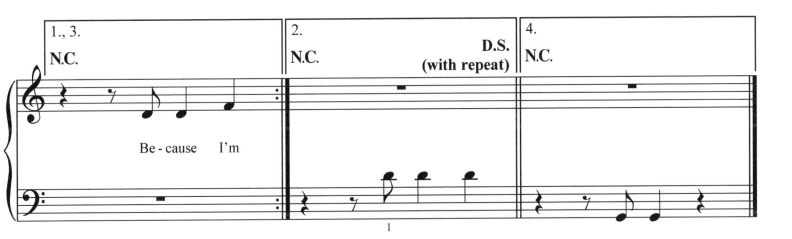

HOME ON THE RANGE

Lyrics by DR. BREWSTER HIGLEY
Music by DAN KELLY

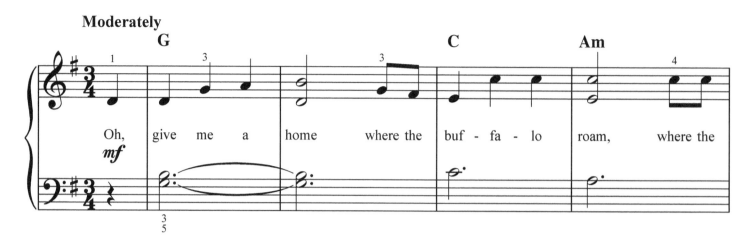

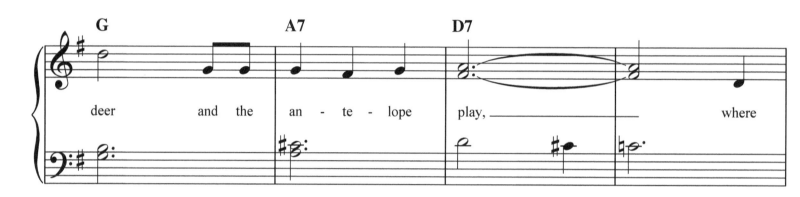

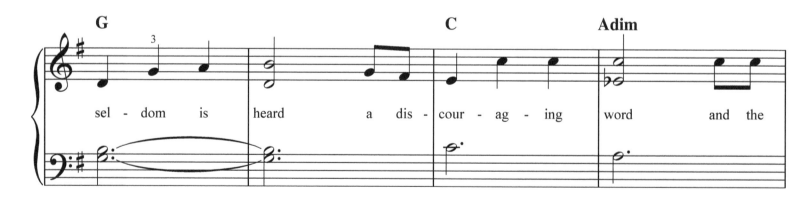

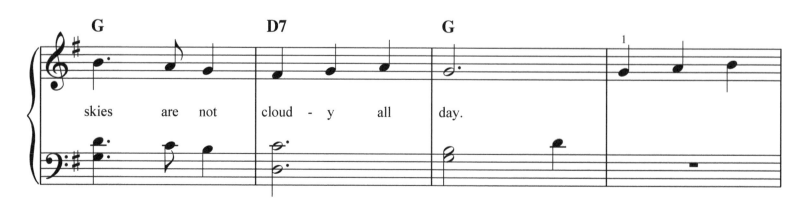

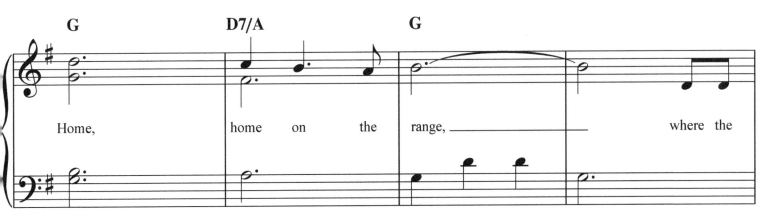

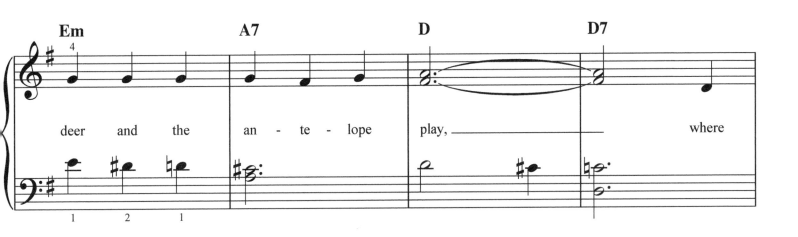

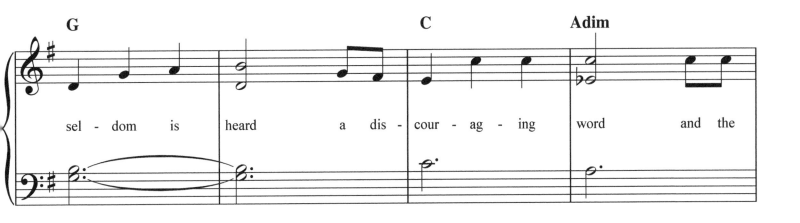

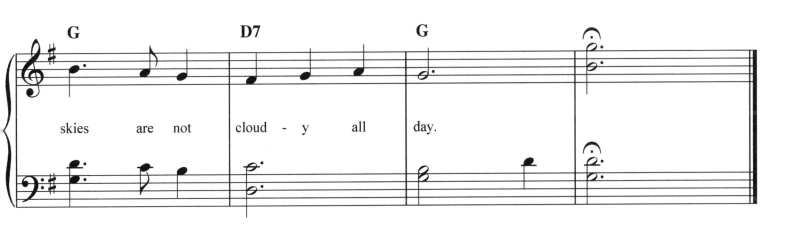

HOW MUCH IS THAT DOGGIE IN THE WINDOW

Words and Music by
BOB MERRILL

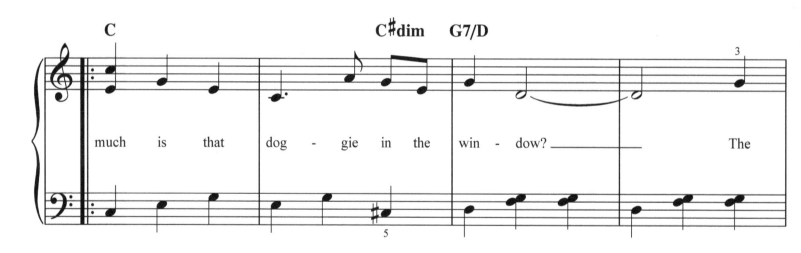

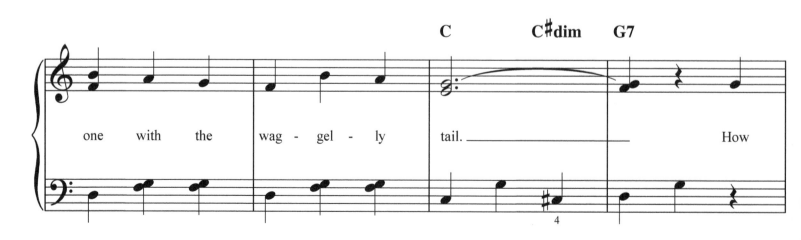

66

I KNOW AN OLD LADY
WHO SWALLOWED A FLY

Traditional

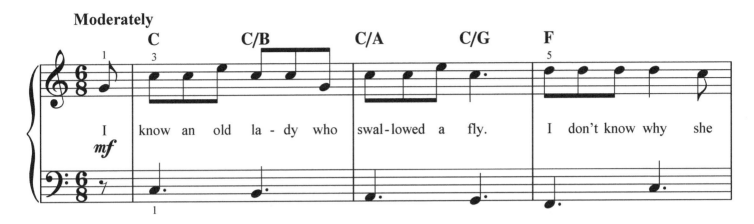

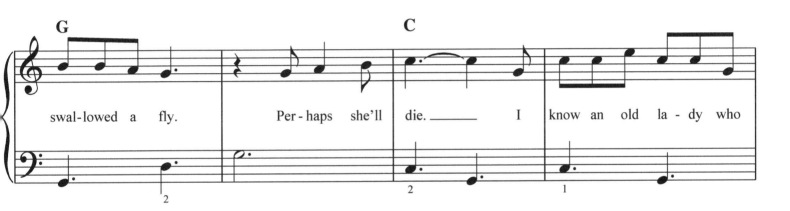

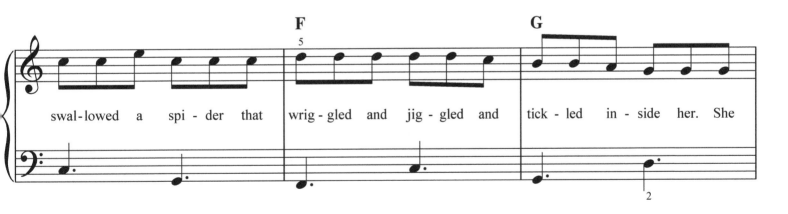

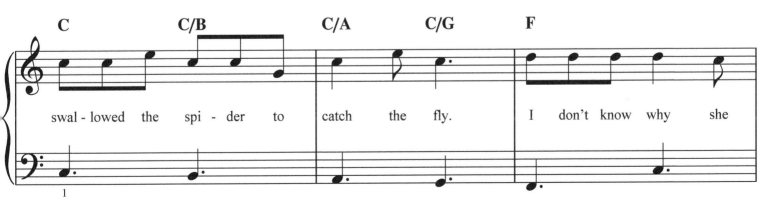

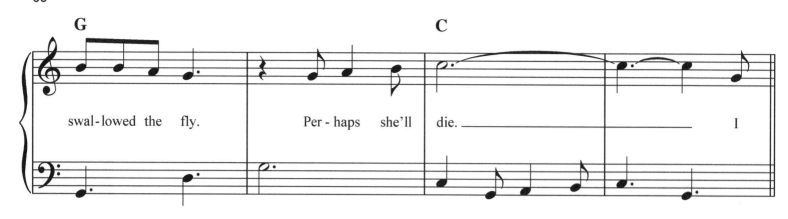

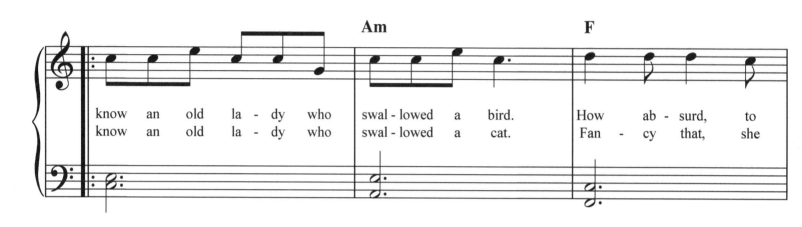

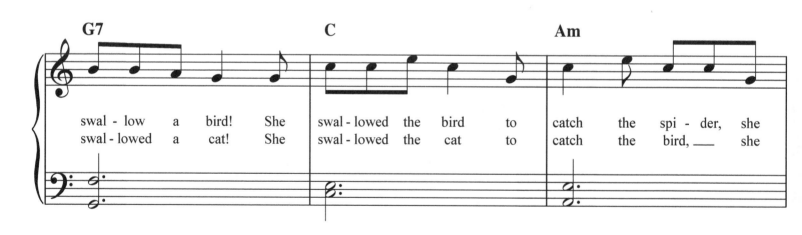

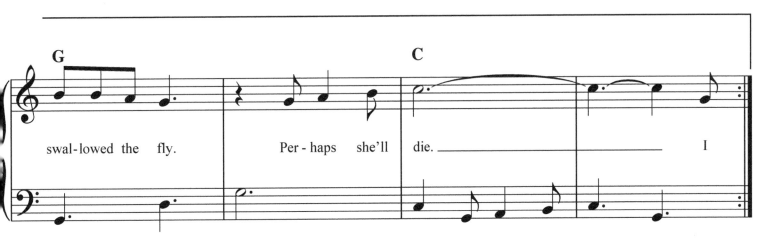

swal-lowed the fly.   Per - haps she'll die. _____ I

swal-lowed the spi - der to   catch   the fly.   I don't know why   she   swal-lowed the fly.

Per - haps she'll   die. _____   I   know an old la - dy who

swal-lowed a horse. _____   She's dead, of course!

I WHISTLE A HAPPY TUNE

from THE KING AND I

Lyrics by OSCAR HAMMERSTEIN II
Music by RICHARD RODGERS

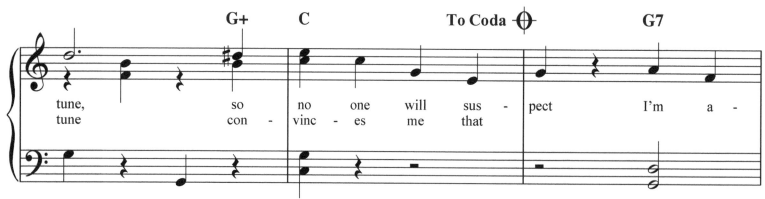

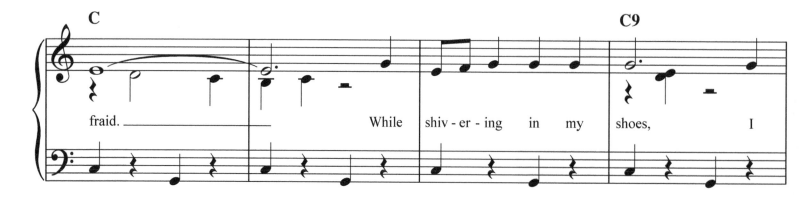

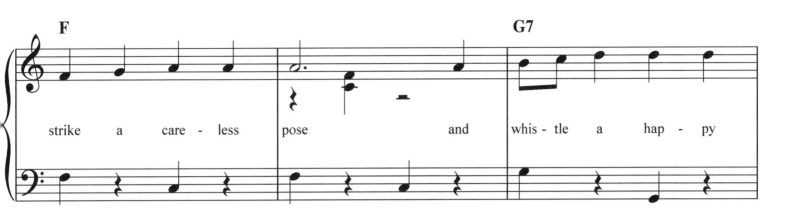

strike a care - less pose and whis - tle a hap - py

tune and no one ev - er knows I'm a - fraid. _____

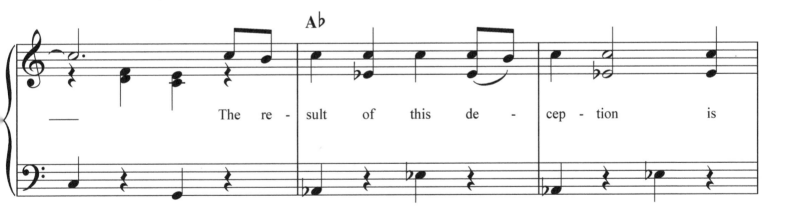

_____ The re - sult of this de - cep - tion is

ver - y strange to ____ tell, for when I fool the

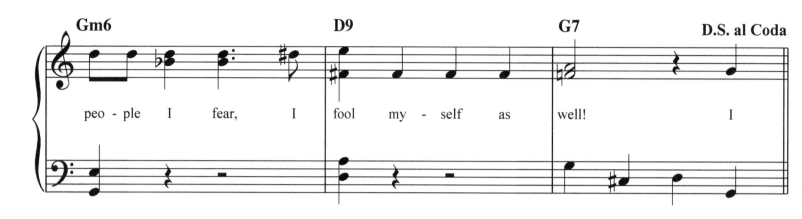

Gm6 **D9** **G7** **D.S. al Coda**

peo - ple I fear, I fool my - self as well! I

CODA **G7** **C**

I'm not a - fraid.

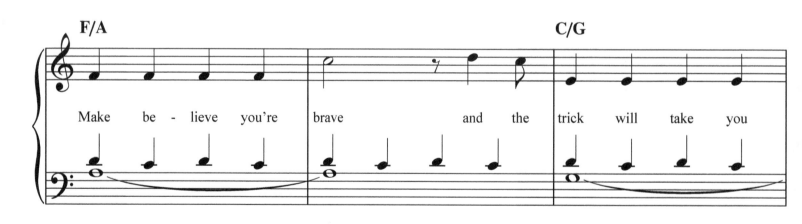

F/A **C/G**

Make be - lieve you're brave and the trick will take you

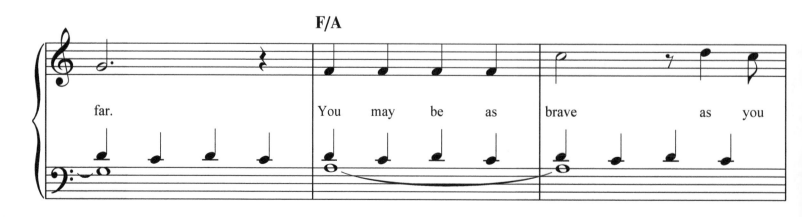

F/A

far. You may be as brave as you

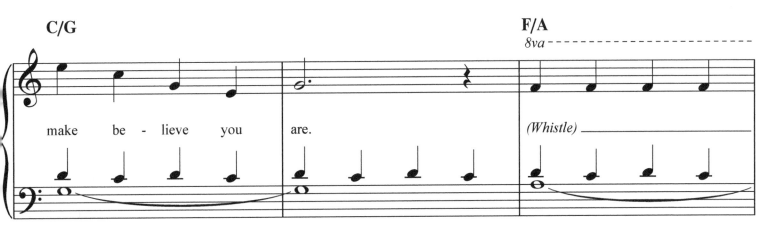

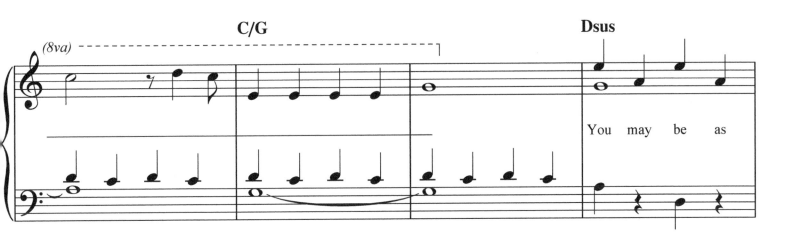

I'LL BE THERE

Words and Music by BERRY GORDY JR.,
HAL DAVIS, WILLIE HUTCH
and BOB WEST

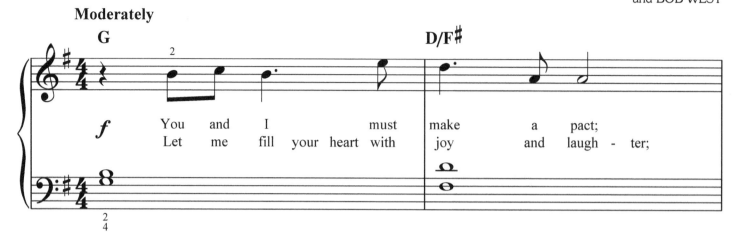

You and I must make a pact;
Let me fill your heart with joy and laugh - ter;

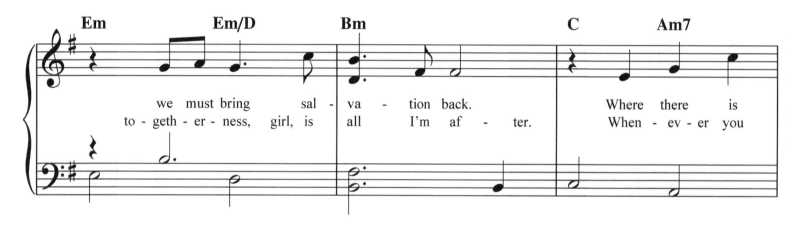

we must bring sal - va - tion back.
to - geth - er - ness, girl, is all I'm af - ter.
Where there is
When - ev - er you

love, I'll be there.
need me, I'll be there.

I'll reach out my hand to you;
I'll be there to pro - tect you
I'll have faith in
with un - self - ish love that

all you do. Just call my name, and I'll be there.
re - spects you. Just call my name; I'll be there.

To Coda

I'll be there to

com-fort you, build my world of dreams a-round you; I'm so glad that I found you.

I'll be there with a love that's strong;_ I'll be your strength, I'll be

IMAGINE

Words and Music by
JOHN LENNON

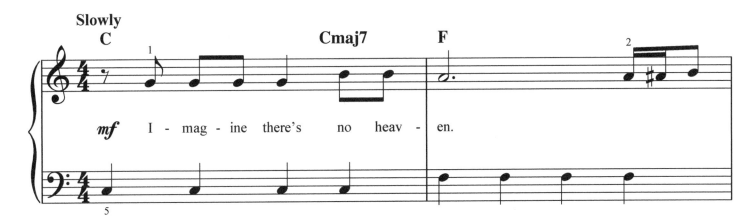

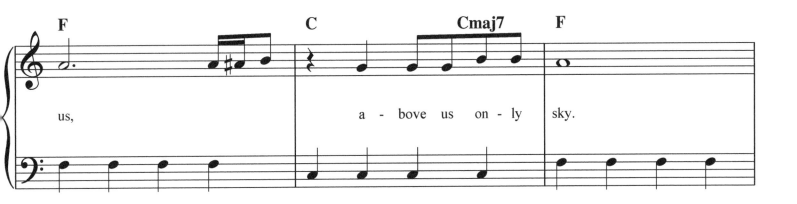

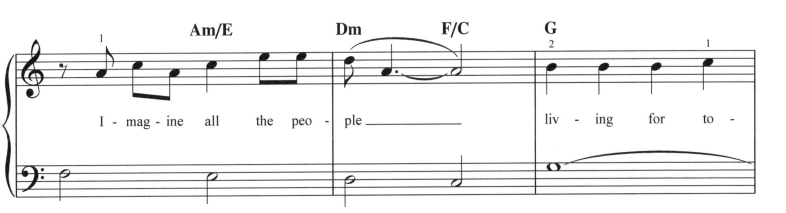

day.   Ah._____   I - mag - ine there's   no   coun - tries.
                                                          sions.

It   is - n't hard   to   do._____   Noth - ing   to   kill   or   die
I   won - der   if   you   can._____   No   need for   greed   or   hun -

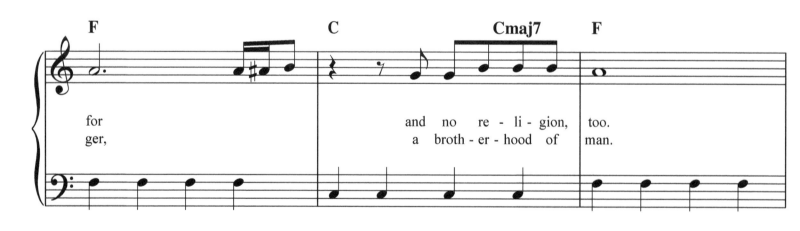

for   and   no   re - li - gion,   too.
ger,   a   broth - er - hood   of   man.

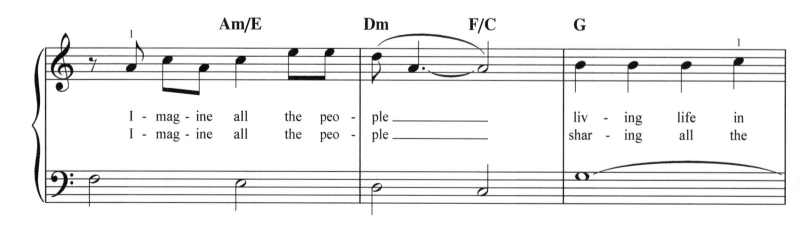

I - mag - ine   all   the   peo - ple_____   liv - ing   life   in
I - mag - ine   all   the   peo - ple_____   shar - ing   all   the

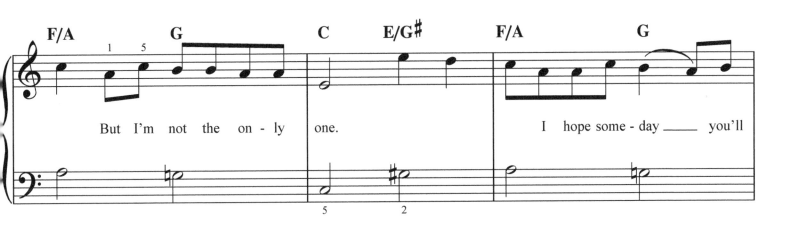

KOOKABURRA
(Kookaburra Sits in the Old Gum Tree)

By MARION SINCLAIR

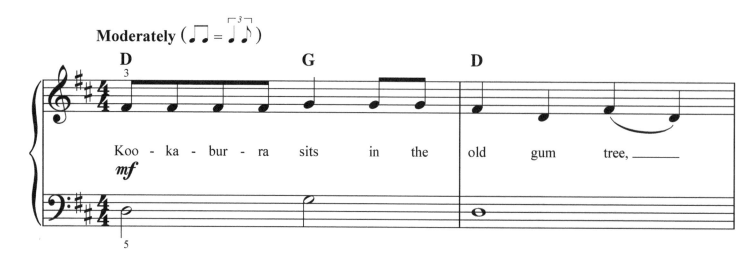

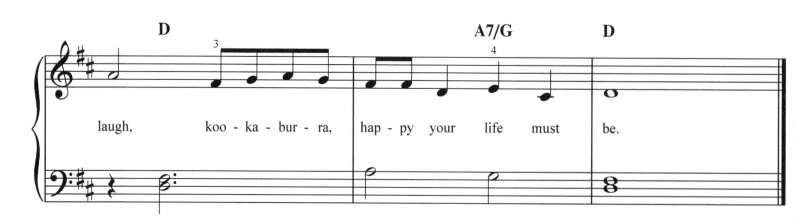

MAGIC PENNY

Words and Music by
MALVINA REYNOLDS

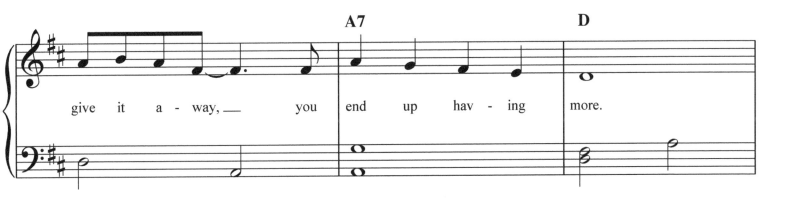

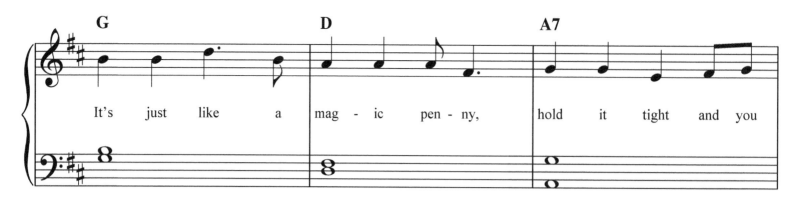

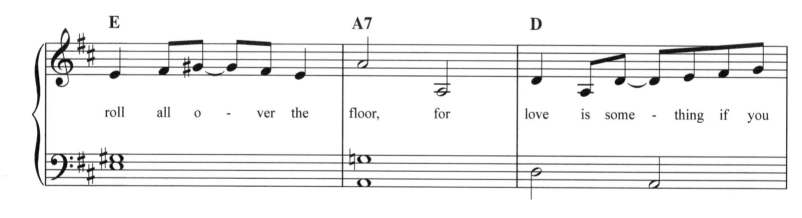

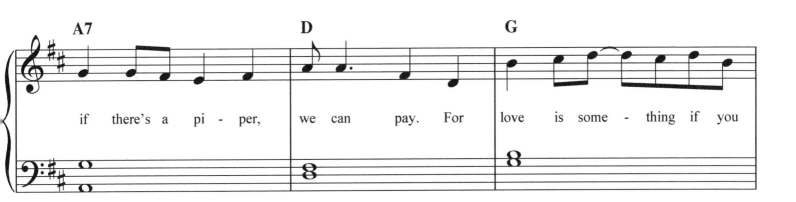

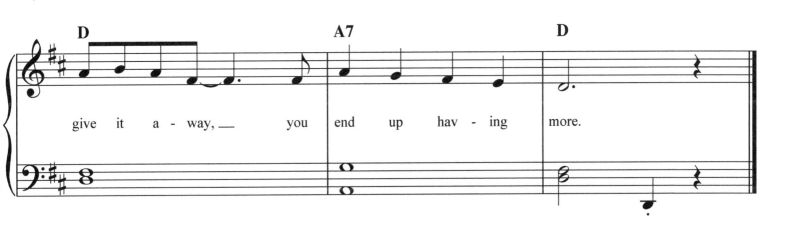

MACARENA

Words and Music by ANTONIO ROMERO
and RAFAEL RUIZ

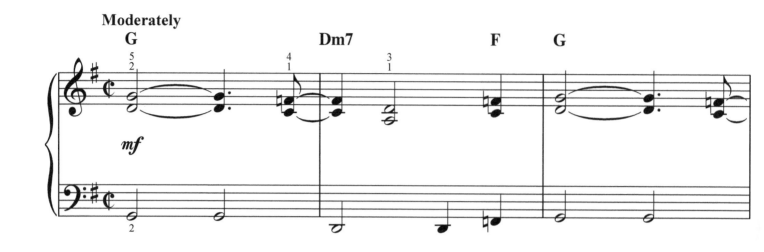

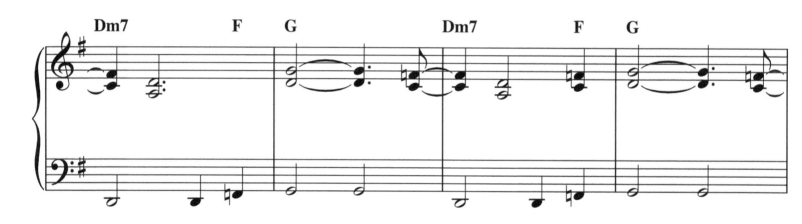

Da - le a tu cuer - po a - le - grí - a Ma - ca - re - na que tu

cuer - po es pá dar - le a - le - gri - a y co - sa bue - na.   Da - le a tu cuer - po a le -

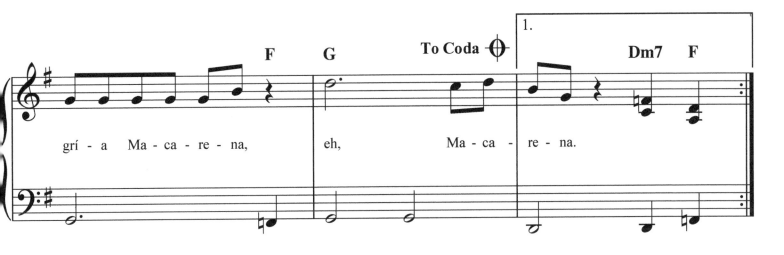

grí - a Ma - ca - re - na,   eh,   Ma - ca - re - na.

re - na.   Ma - ca - re - na tie - ne un no - vio que se lla - ma,   que se

lla - ma, de a - pe - lli - do Vi - to - ri - no.   Y en la ju - ra de ban - de - ra del mu -

cha - cho   se   la   dió con dos a - mi - gos.   Ma - ca -

re - na   tie - ne un   no - vio que   se   lla - ma,   que   se

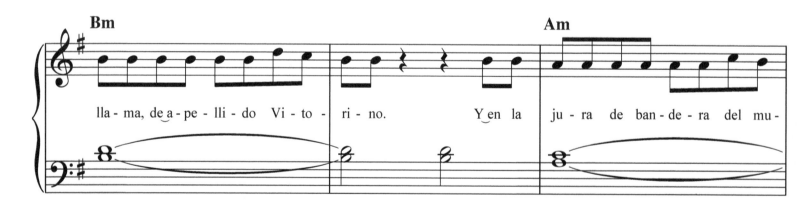

lla - ma, de a - pe - lli - do   Vi - to -   ri - no.   Y en la   ju - ra de ban - de - ra del mu -

cha - cho   se   la   dió con dos a - mi - gos.

CODA

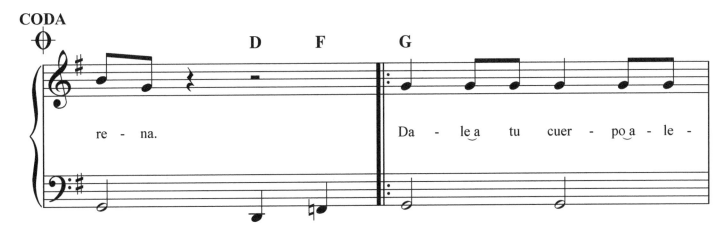

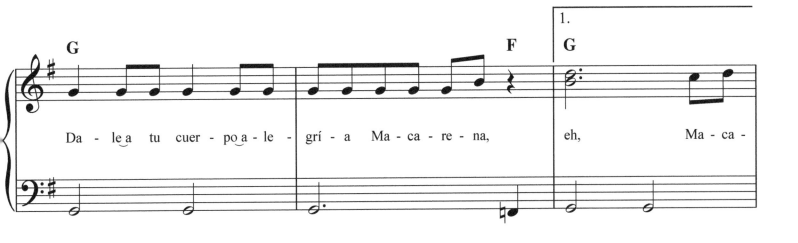

MAKE NEW FRIENDS

Traditional

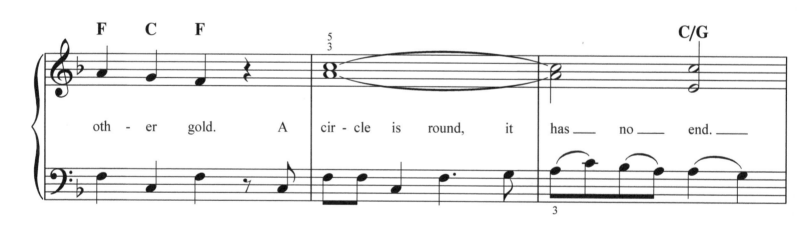

MORE WE GET TOGETHER

German Folk Song

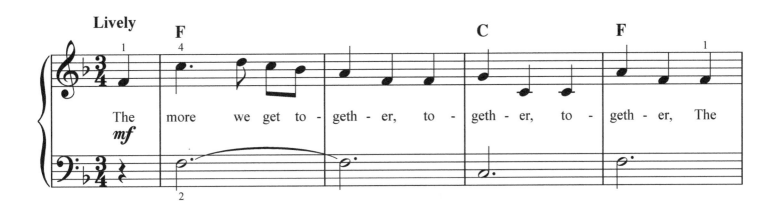

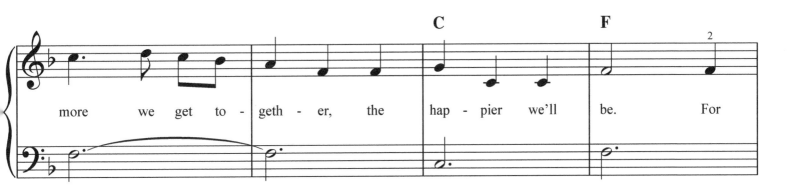

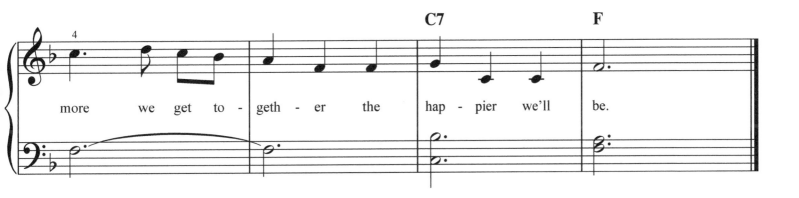

THE NAME GAME

Words and Music by LINCOLN CHASE
and SHIRLEY ELLISTON

let's play a game. _____ I bet - cha I can make a rhyme _____

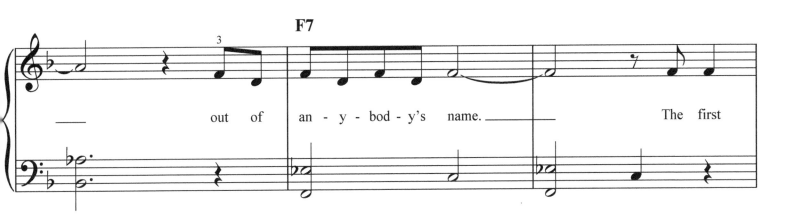

_____ out of an - y - bod - y's name. _____ The first

let - ter of the name, _____ I treat it like it was - n't there. _____

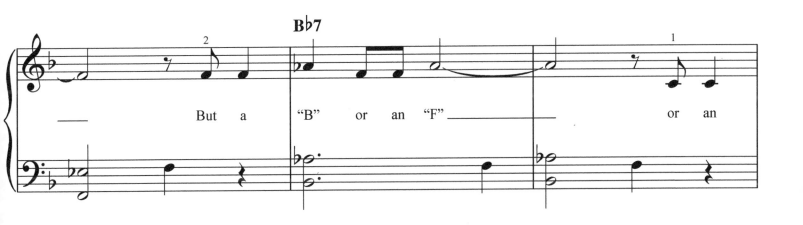

_____ But a "B" or an "F" _____ or an

"M" will ap - pear. And then I say "Bo," add a "B," then I
"Bo," add a "B," now

say the name, then "Bo - na - na, fan - na" and "fo." And then I
To - ny with a "B," now "Bo - na - na, fan - na" and "fo." And now you

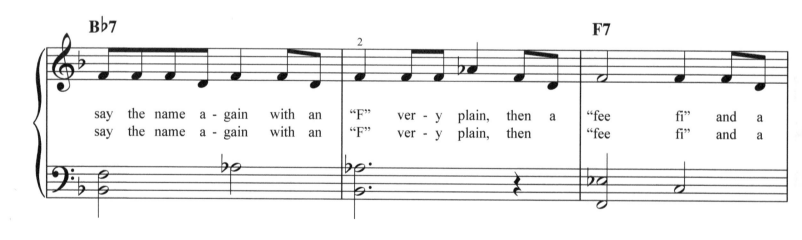

say the name a - gain with an "F" ver - y plain, then a "fee fi" and a
say the name a - gain with an "F" ver - y plain, then "fee fi" and a

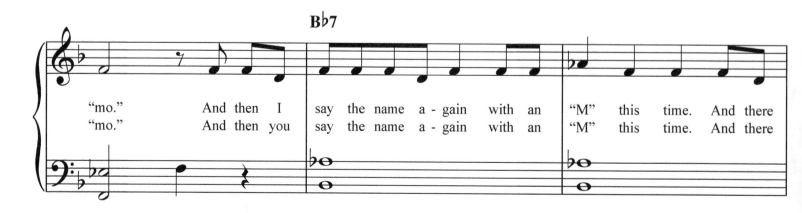

"mo." And then I say the name a - gain with an "M" this time. And there
"mo." And then you say the name a - gain with an "M" this time. And there

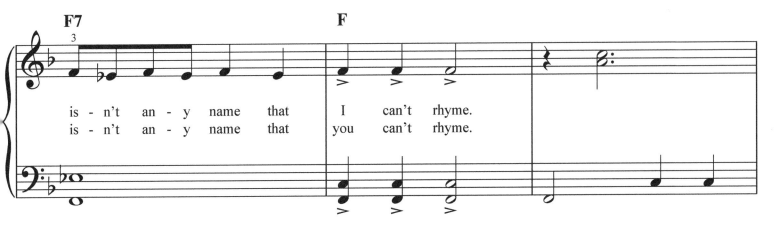

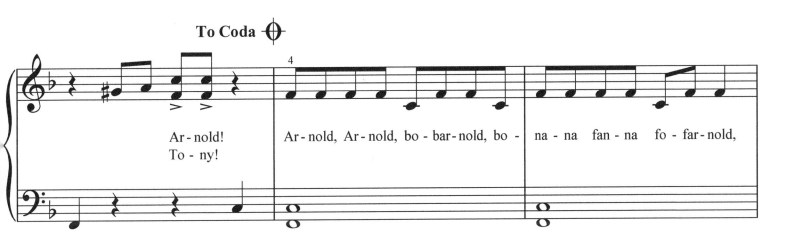

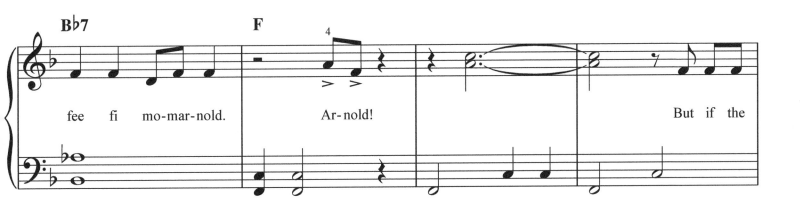

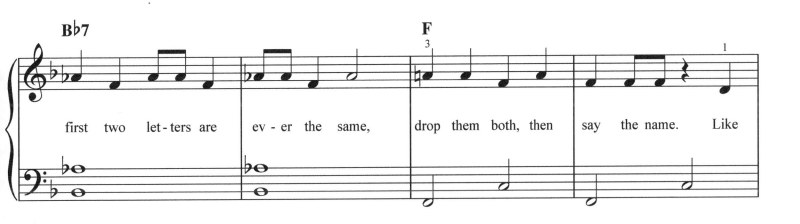

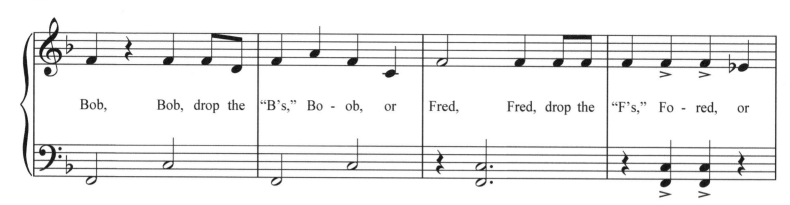

Bob,   Bob, drop the "B's," Bo - ob,   or   Fred,   Fred, drop the "F's," Fo - red,   or

B♭7   **F**

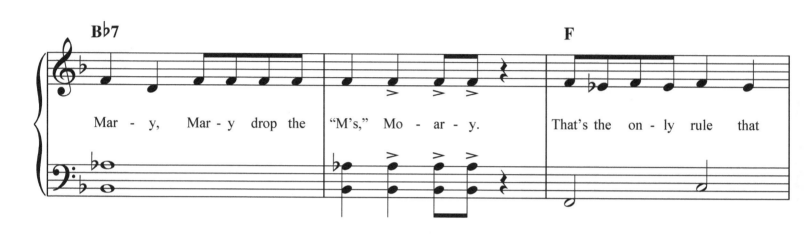

Mar - y,   Mar - y drop the   "M's," Mo - ar - y.   That's the on - ly rule that

D.S. al Coda

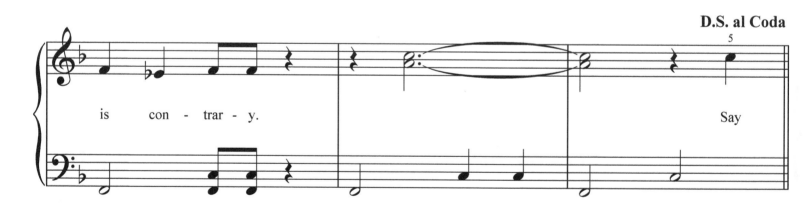

is   con - trar - y.   Say

CODA

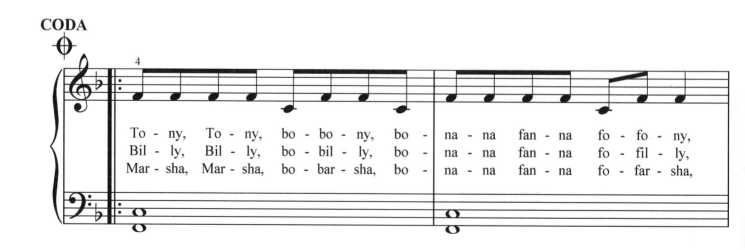

To - ny,   To - ny,   bo - bo - ny,   bo - na - na fan - na   fo - fo - ny,
Bil - ly,   Bil - ly,   bo - bil - ly,   bo - na - na fan - na   fo - fil - ly,
Mar - sha,   Mar - sha,   bo - bar - sha,   bo - na - na fan - na   fo - far - sha,

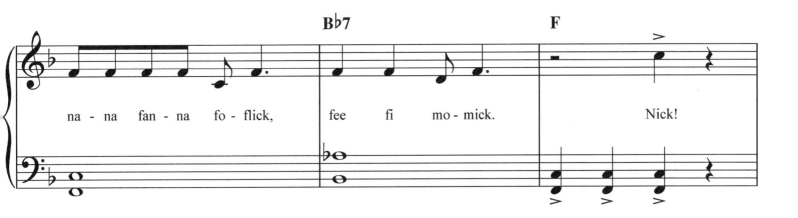

NEVER SMILE AT A CROCODILE

from PETER PAN

Words by JACK LAWRENCE
Music by FRANK CHURCHILL

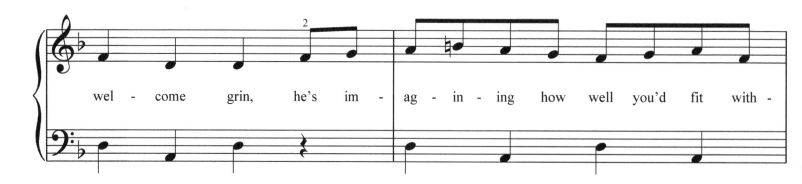

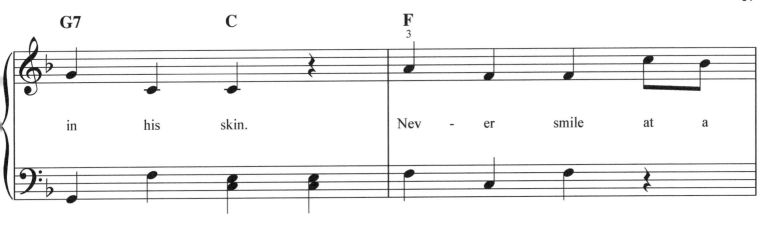

G7   C   F

in   his   skin.   Nev - er   smile   at   a

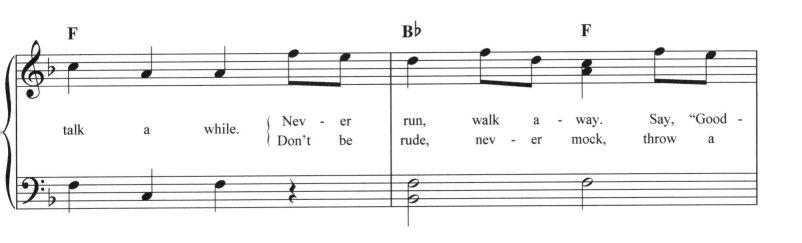

B♭

croc - o - dile,   nev - er   tip   your   hat   and   stop   to

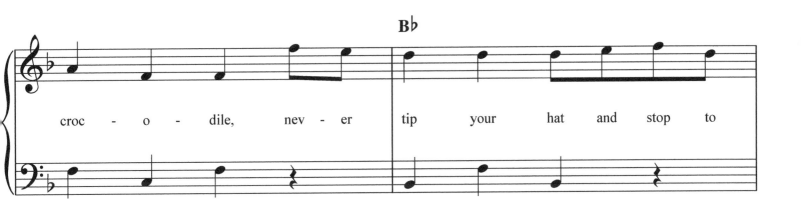

F   B♭   F

talk   a   while.   { Nev - er   run,   walk   a - way.   Say, "Good -
Don't   be   rude,   nev - er   mock,   throw   a

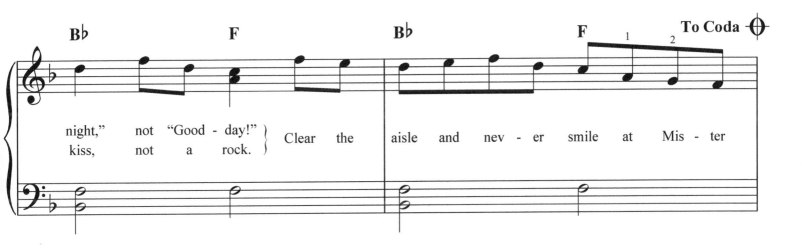

B♭   F   B♭   F   1   2   **To Coda** ⊕

night,"   not   "Good - day!" } Clear   the   aisle   and   nev - er   smile   at   Mis - ter
kiss,   not   a   rock.

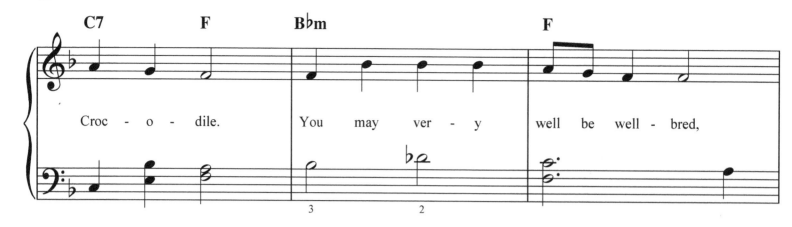

Croc - o - dile. You may ver - y well be well - bred,

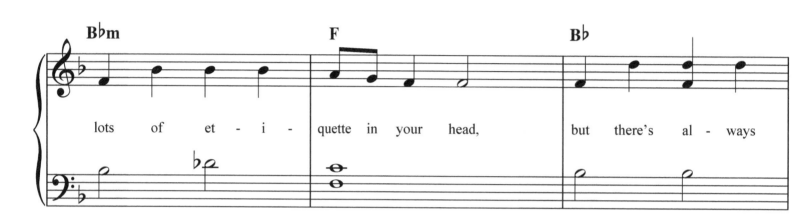

lots of et - i - quette in your head, but there's al - ways

D.S. al Coda

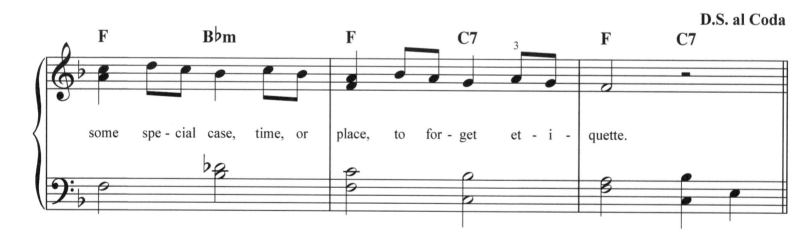

some spe - cial case, time, or place, to for - get et - i - quette.

CODA

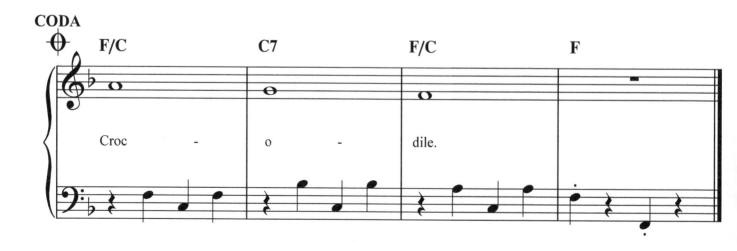

Croc - o - dile.

OH WHERE, OH WHERE HAS MY LITTLE DOG GONE

Words by SEP. WINNER
Traditional Melody

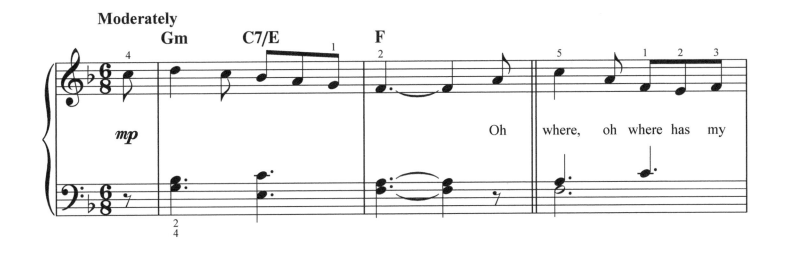

OLD MacDONALD

Traditional Children's Song

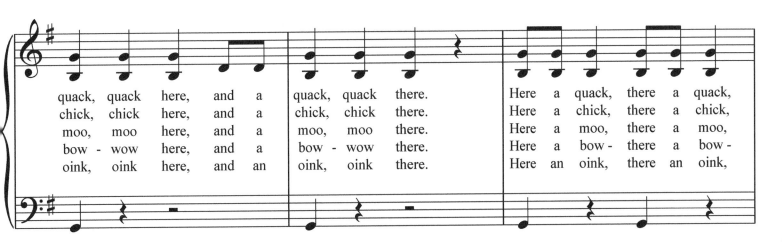

quack, quack here, and a   quack, quack there.   Here a quack, there a quack,
chick, chick here, and a   chick, chick there.   Here a chick, there a chick,
moo, moo here, and a   moo, moo there.   Here a moo, there a moo,
bow - wow here, and a   bow - wow there.   Here a bow - there a bow -
oink, oink here, and an   oink, oink there.   Here an oink, there an oink,

G/B   **C**   **G/D**

ev - 'ry - where a quack, quack.
ev - 'ry - where a chick, chick.
ev - 'ry - where a moo, moo.   Old Mac - Don - ald   had a farm,
ev - 'ry - where a bow - wow.
ev - 'ry - where an oink, oink.

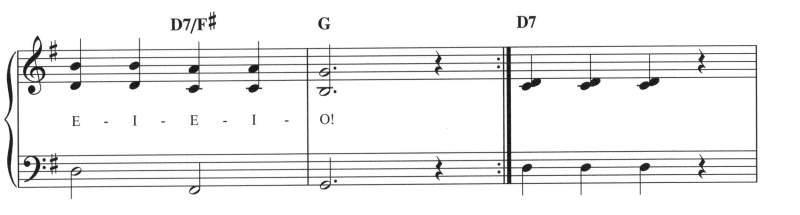

D7/F♯   **G**   **D7**

E - I - E - I - O!

D7/F♯   **G**

POP GOES THE WEASEL

Traditional

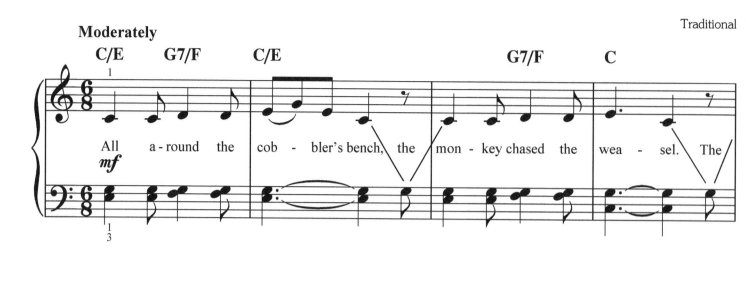

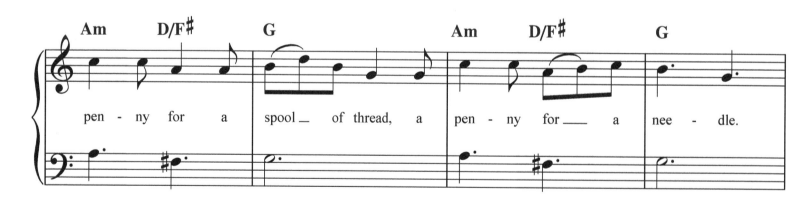

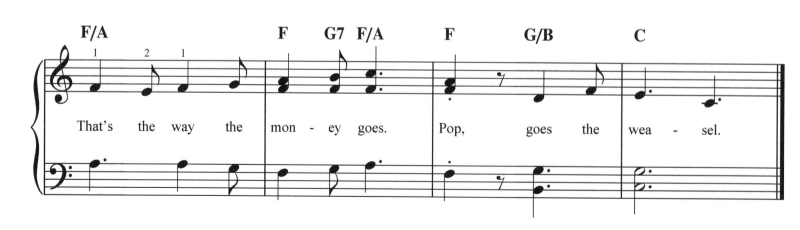

PURPLE PEOPLE EATER™

Words and Music by
SHEB WOOLEY®

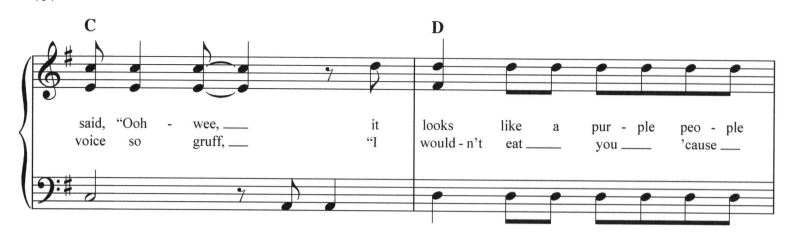

said, "Ooh - wee, ___ it
voice so gruff, ___ "I
looks like a pur - ple peo - ple
would - n't eat ___ you ___ 'cause ___

Chorus

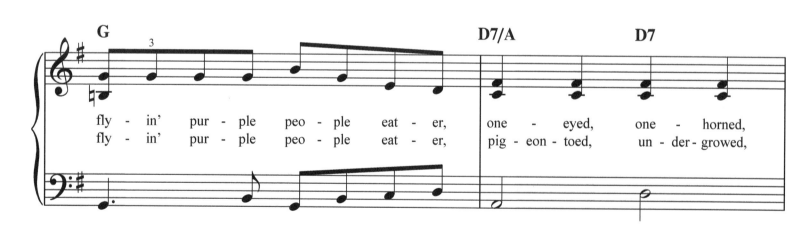

eat - er to me." ___ 1.,2. It was a
you're ___ so tough." ___ 3.–5. Well,
one - eyed, one - horned,
bless my soul, rock 'n roll,

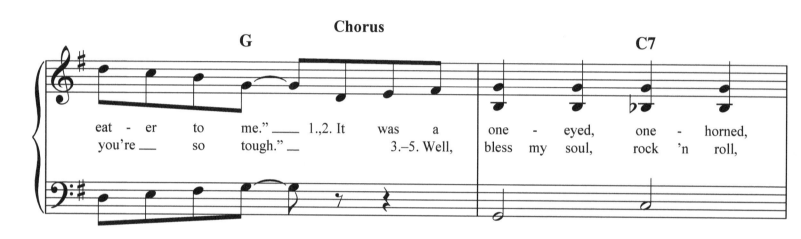

fly - in' pur - ple peo - ple eat - er,
fly - in' pur - ple peo - ple eat - er,
one - eyed, one - horned,
pig - eon - toed, un - der - growed,

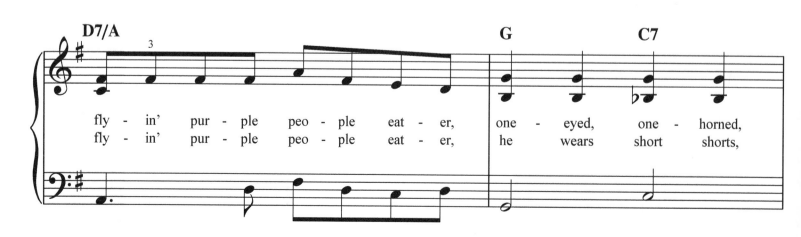

fly - in' pur - ple peo - ple eat - er,
fly - in' pur - ple peo - ple eat - er,
one - eyed, one - horned,
he wears short shorts,

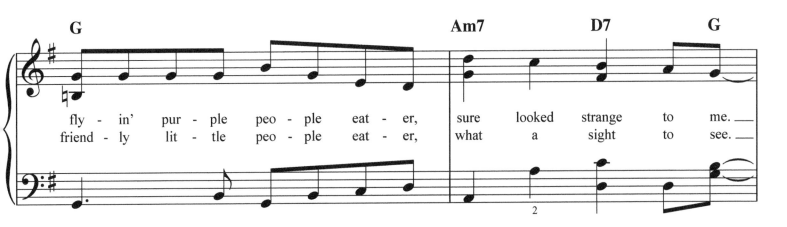

Additional Lyrics

3. I said, "Mister purple people eater, what's your line?"
   He said, "Eatin' purple people, and it sure is fine,
   But that's not the reason that I came to land,
   I wanna get a job in a rock 'n' roll band."
   Chorus

4. And then he swung from the tree and he lit on the ground,
   And he started to rock, a-really rockin' around.
   It was a crazy ditty with a swingin' tune,
   Singa bop bapa loop a lap a loom bam boom.
   Chorus

5. Well, he went on his way and then what-a you know,
   I saw him last night on a T.V. show.
   He was blowin' it out, really knockin' 'em dead.
   Playin' rock 'n' roll music through the horn of his head.
   Chorus

THE RHYME OF THE CHIVALROUS SHARK

Words and Music by
WALLACE IRWIN

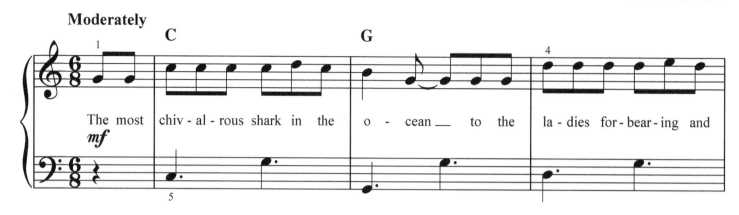

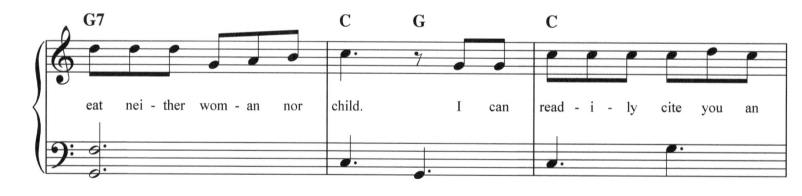

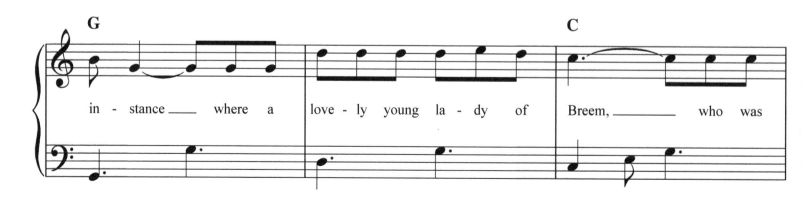

ROCKIN' ROBIN

Words and Music by
J. THOMAS

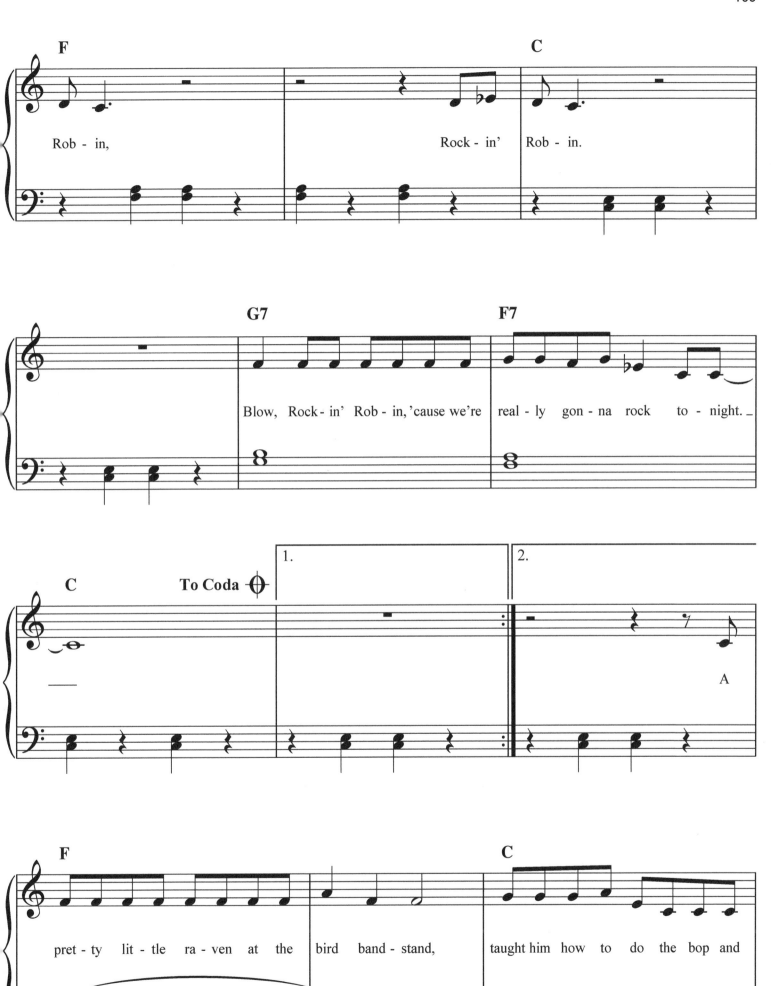

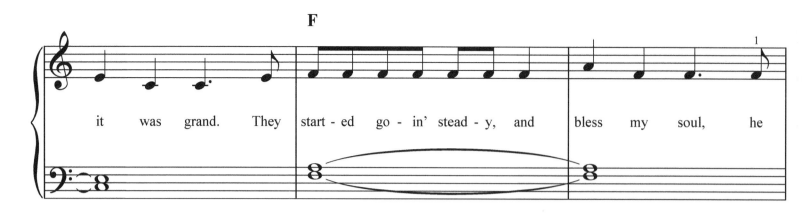

it was grand. They start-ed go-in' stead-y, and bless my soul, he

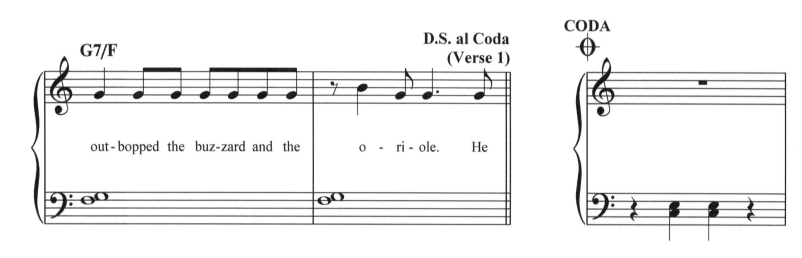

G7/F

out-bopped the buz-zard and the o - ri - ole. He

D.S. al Coda
(Verse 1)

CODA

F G C

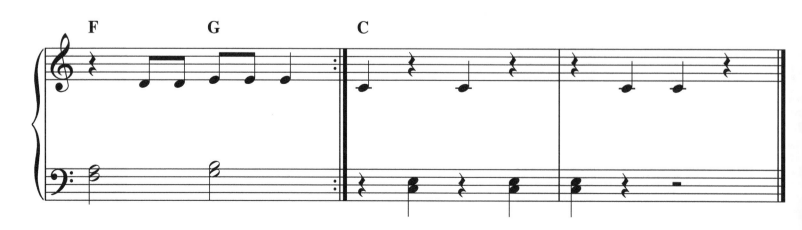

F G C

SHE'LL BE COMIN' 'ROUND THE MOUNTAIN

Traditional

ROW, ROW, ROW YOUR BOAT

Traditional

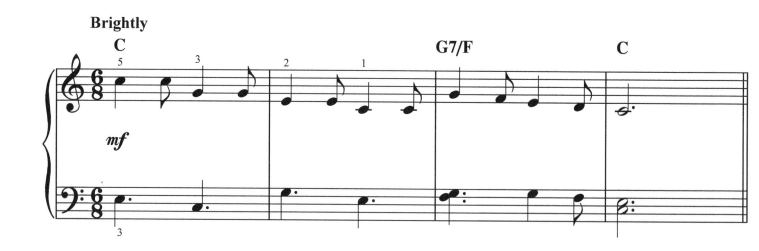

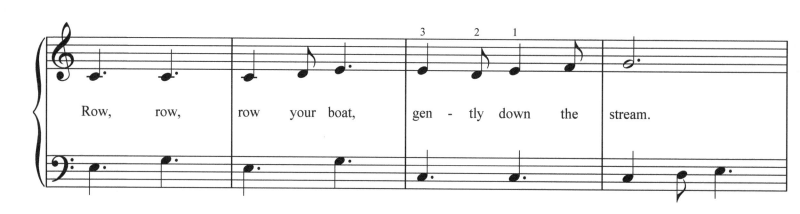

Row, row, row your boat, gen - tly down the stream.

Mer - ri - ly, mer - ri - ly, mer - ri - ly, mer - ri - ly. Life is but a

dream.   Row,   row,   row your boat,   gen - tly down the

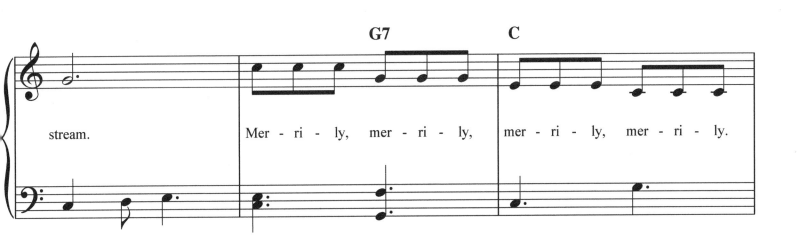

stream.   Mer - ri - ly, mer - ri - ly,   mer - ri - ly, mer - ri - ly.

Life is but a dream.

SHAKE IT OFF

Words and Music by TAYLOR SWIFT,
MAX MARTIN and SHELLBACK

at least, that's what peo - ple say, _____ mm, mm. That's what peo - ple
And that's what they don't know, _____ mm, mm. That's what they don't

say, _____ mm, mm. But I keep cruis - ing;
know, _____ mm, mm. But I keep cruis - ing;

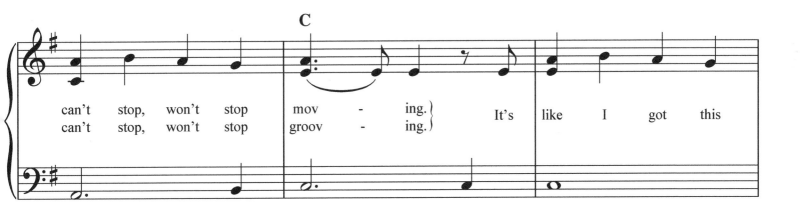

can't stop, won't stop mov - ing. } It's like I got this
can't stop, won't stop groov - ing. }

mu - sic in my mind say - ing, "It's gon - na be al - right." _

'Cause the play - ers gon - na play, play, play, play, play and the

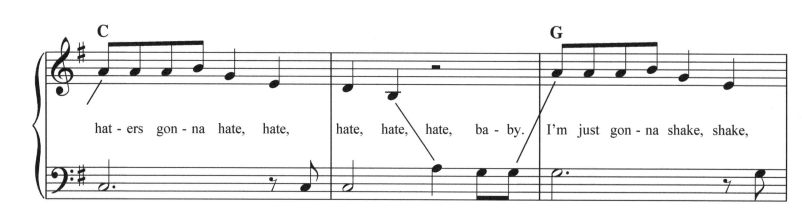

hat - ers gon - na hate, hate, hate, hate, hate, ba - by. I'm just gon - na shake, shake,

shake, shake, shake; I shake it off, I shake it off. (Ooh, __ ooh!) Heart -

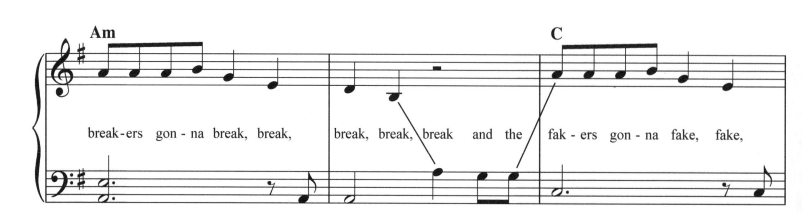

break - ers gon - na break, break, break, break, break and the fak - ers gon - na fake, fake,

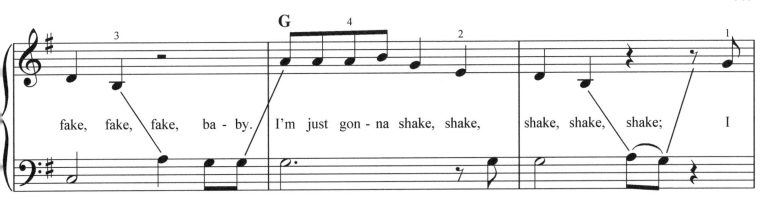

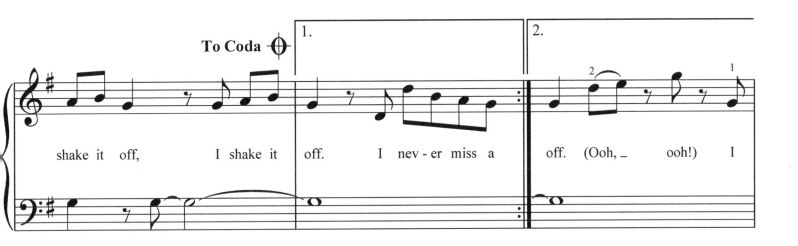

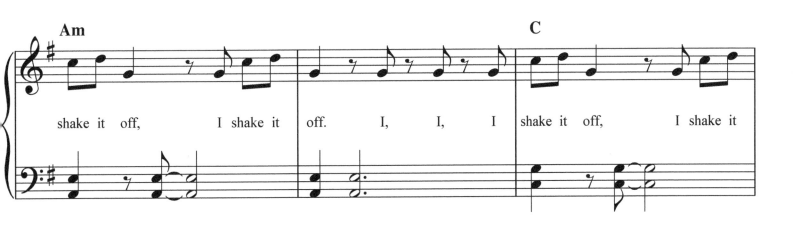

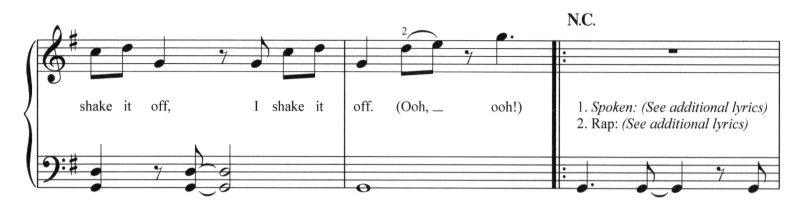

shake it off, I shake it off. (Ooh, ___ ooh!)

N.C.

1. *Spoken: (See additional lyrics)*
2. Rap: *(See additional lyrics)*

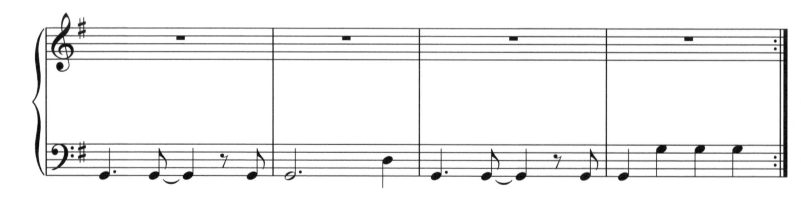

D.S. al Coda

Rap ends Yeah, ___ oh. _____ 'Cause the

CODA

off. (Ooh, ___ ooh!) I

119

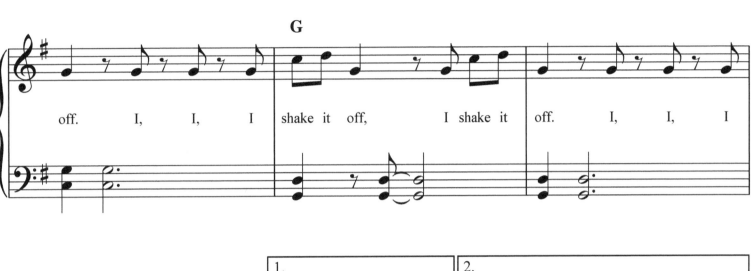

Additional Lyrics

Spoken: *Hey, hey, hey! Just think: While you've been getting*
Down and out about the liars and the dirty, dirty
Cheats of the world, you could've been getting down to
This. Sick. Beat!

Rap: My ex-man brought his new girlfriend.
She's like, "Oh, my god!" But I'm just gonna shake.
And to the fella over there with the hella good hair,
Won't you come on over, baby? We can shake, shake, shake.

SIX LITTLE DUCKS

Traditional

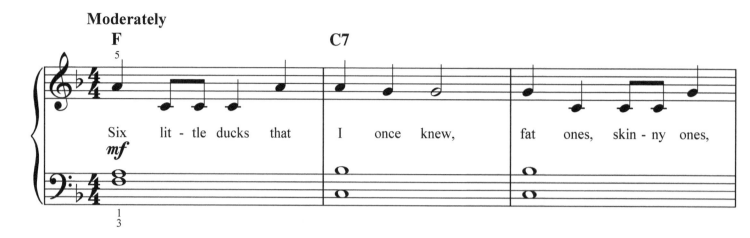

Moderately

Six lit - tle ducks that I once knew, fat ones, skin - ny ones,

fair ones too. But the one lit - tle duck with the feath - er on his back,

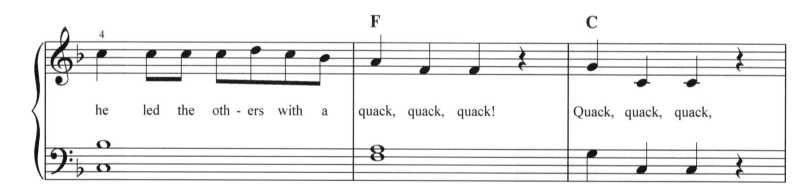

he led the oth - ers with a quack, quack, quack! Quack, quack, quack,

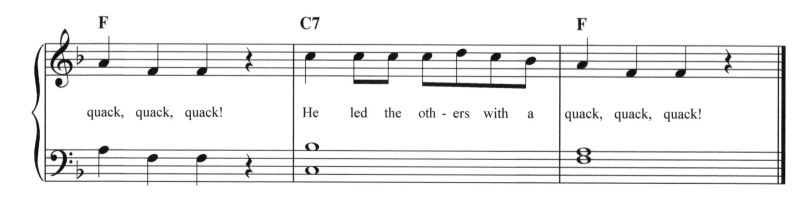

quack, quack, quack! He led the oth - ers with a quack, quack, quack!

WE ARE FAMILY

Words and Music by NILE RODGERS
and BERNARD EDWARDS

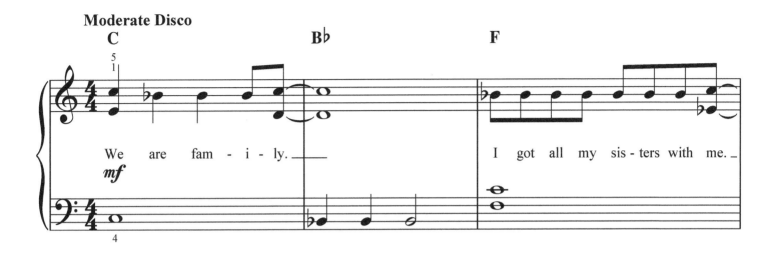

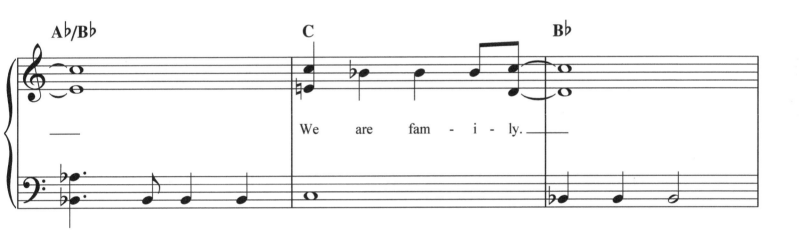

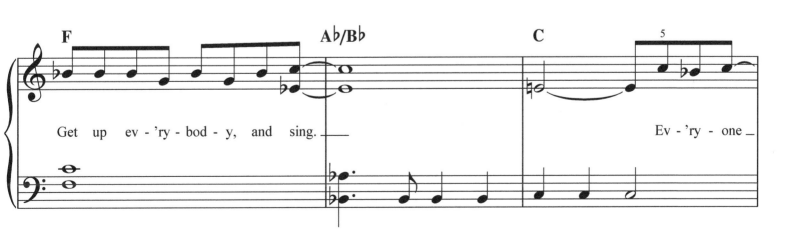

can see ___ we're to geth - er ___ as we walk ___ on by. ___

And we flock ___ just like birds ___ of a feath - er; ___ I won't tell ___

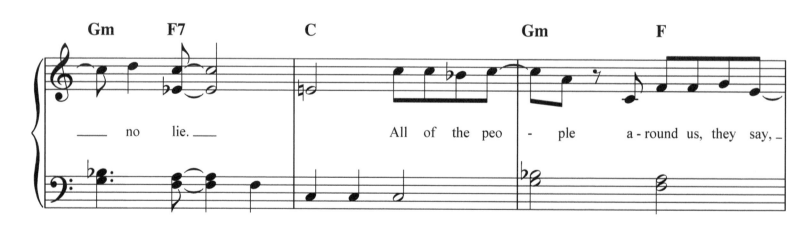

___ no lie. ___ All of the peo - ple a - round us, they say, ___

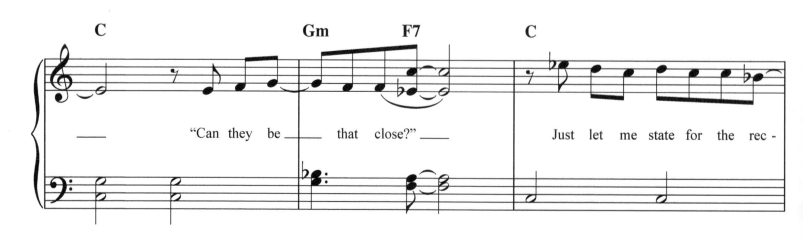

___ "Can they be ___ that close?" ___ Just let me state for the rec -

-ord: We're giv-ing love in a fam - 'ly dose.

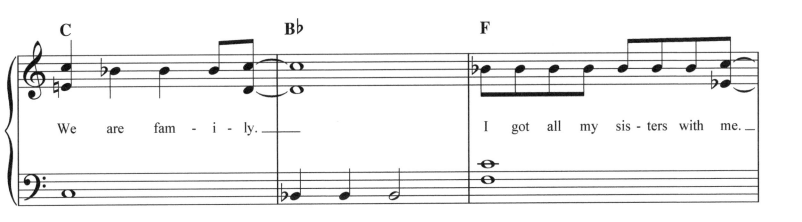

We are fam - i - ly. I got all my sis-ters with me.

We are fam - i - ly.

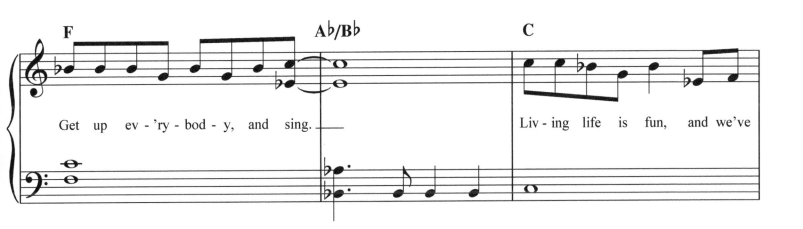

Get up ev-'ry-bod - y, and sing. Liv-ing life is fun, and we've

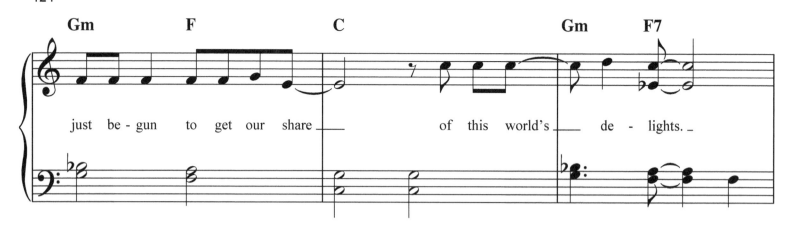

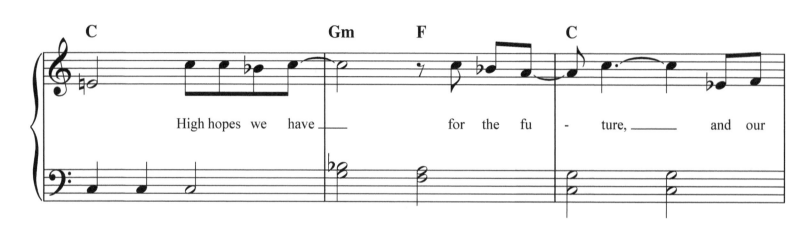

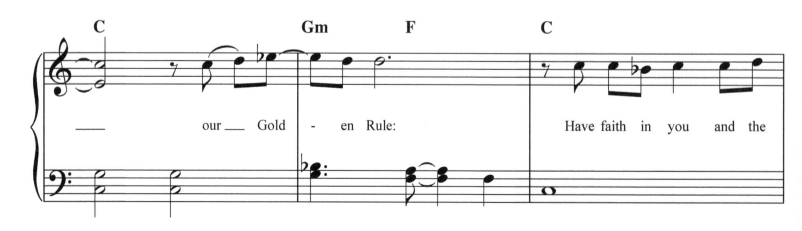

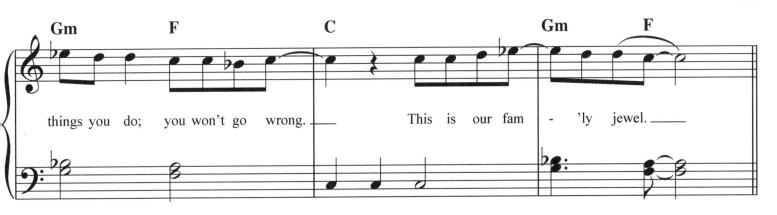

things you do; you won't go wrong. This is our fam - 'ly jewel.

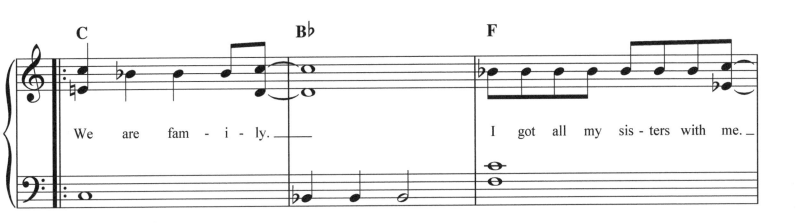

We are fam - i - ly. I got all my sis - ters with me.

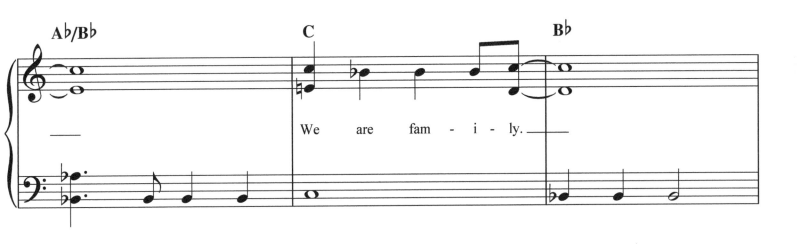

We are fam - i - ly.

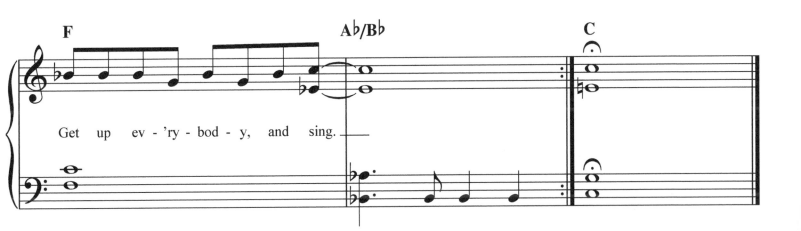

Get up ev - 'ry - bod - y, and sing.

TRY EVERYTHING

from ZOOTOPIA

Words and Music by SIA FURLER,
TOR ERIK HERMANSEN and MIKKEL ERIKSEN

Moderate Dance beat

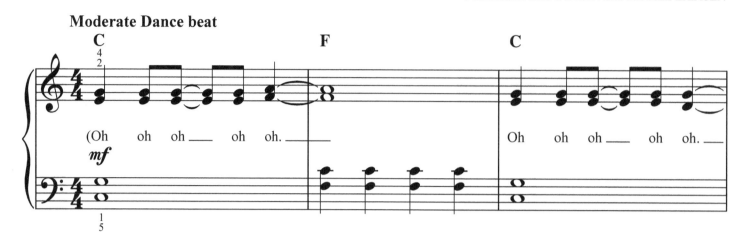

(Oh oh oh ___ oh oh. ___

Oh oh oh ___ oh oh. ___

Oh oh oh ___ oh oh.

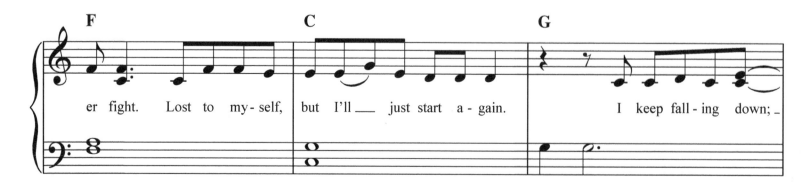

Oh oh oh ___ oh oh.) ___ I messed up to-night. ___ I lost an-oth-

er fight. Lost to my-self, but I'll ___ just start a-gain. I keep fall-ing down; ___

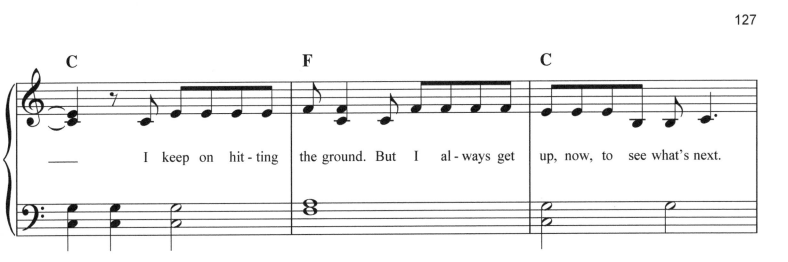

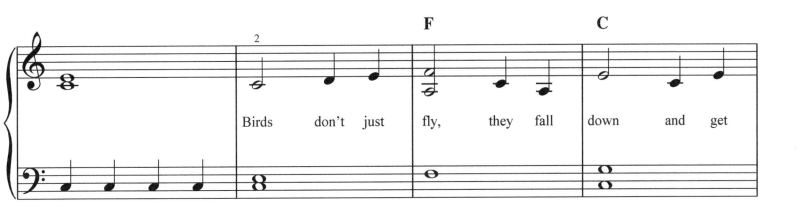

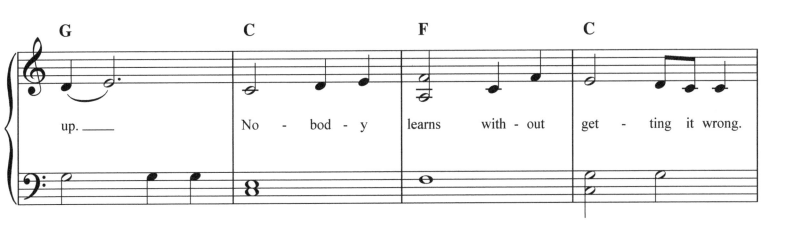

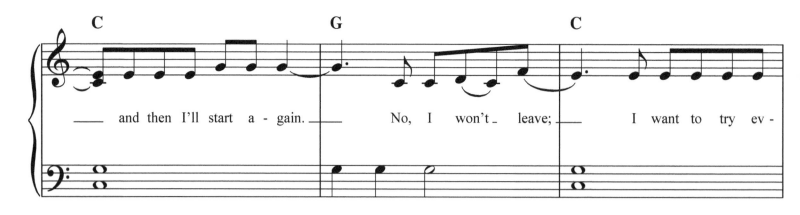

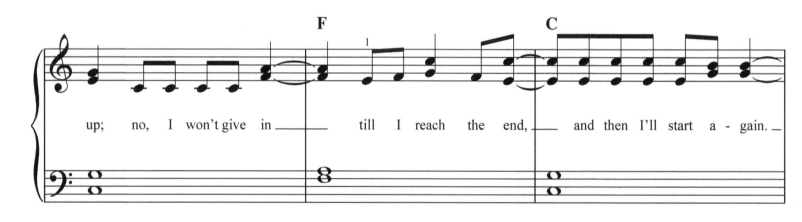

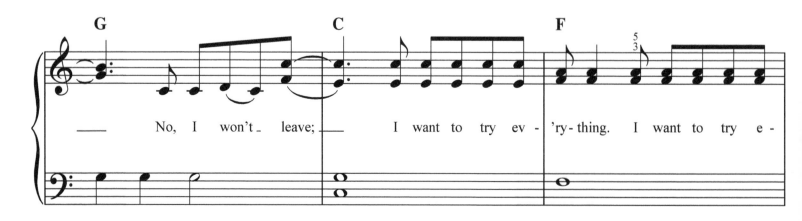

TWIST AND SHOUT

Words and Music by BERT RUSSELL
and PHIL MEDLEY

Moderately, with a beat

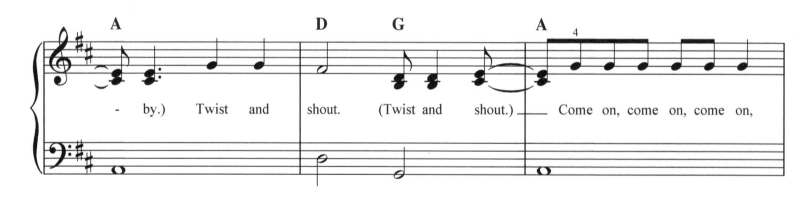

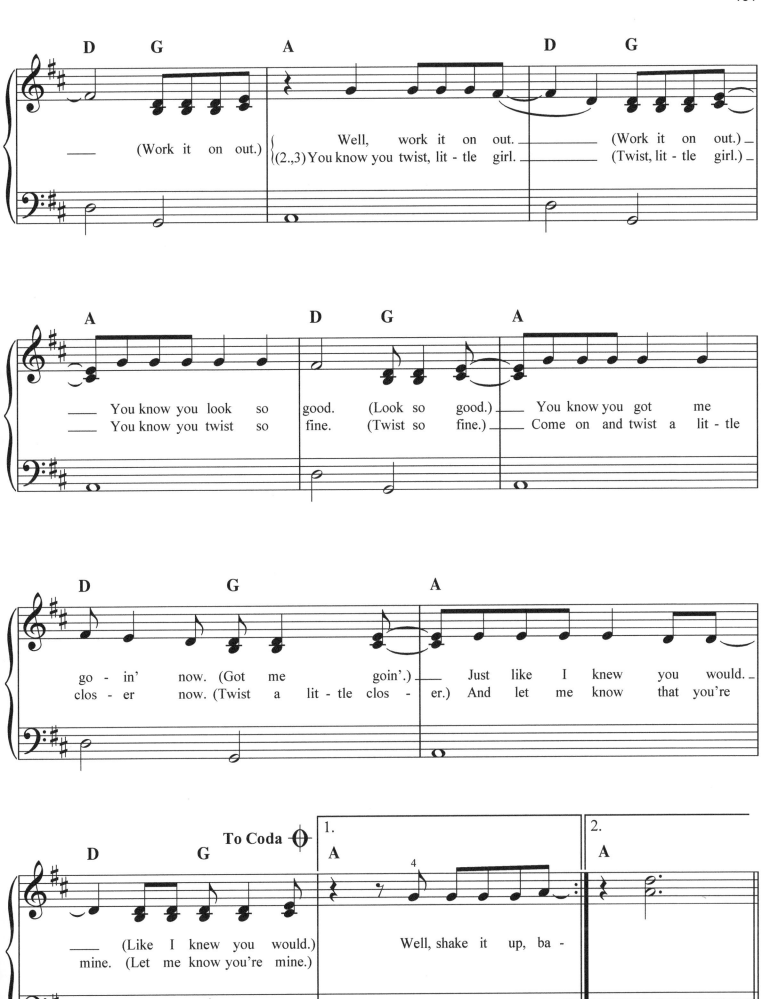

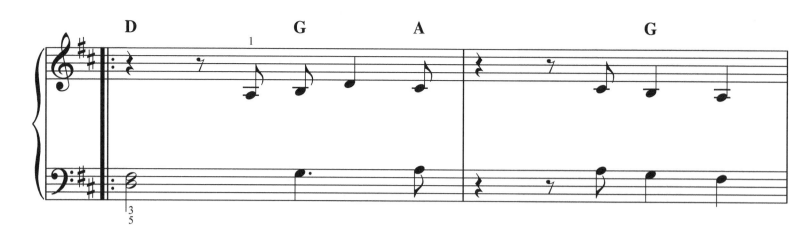

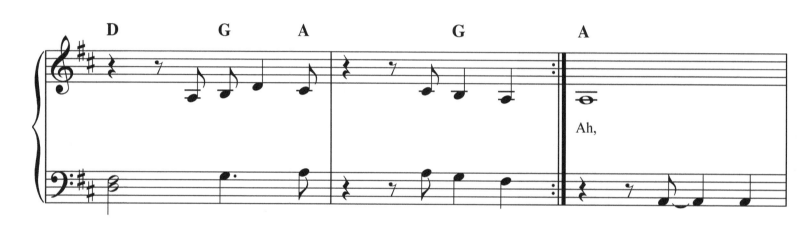

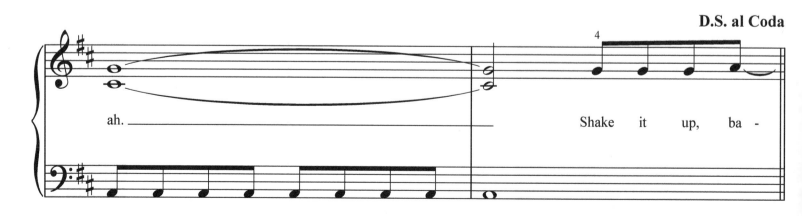

CODA

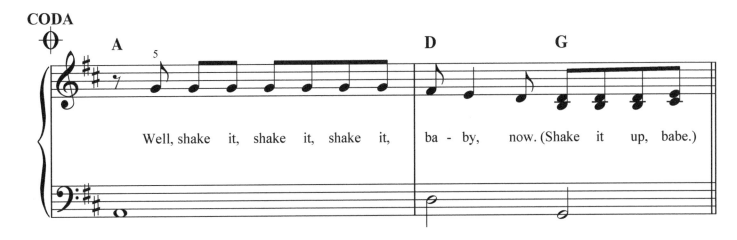

Well, shake it, shake it, shake it, ba - by, now. (Shake it up, babe.)

Well, shake it, shake it, shake it ba - by, now. (Shake it up, babe.)

Oo.   Ah,   ah,

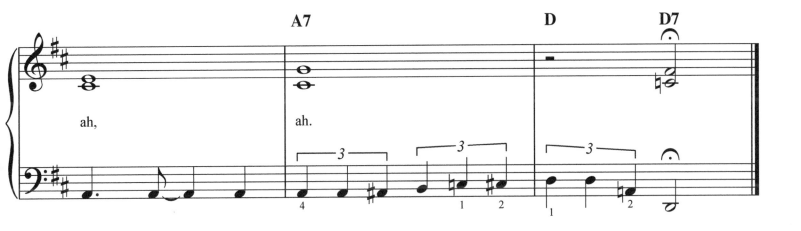

ah,   ah.

YELLOW SUBMARINE

Words and Music by JOHN LENNON
and PAUL McCARTNEY

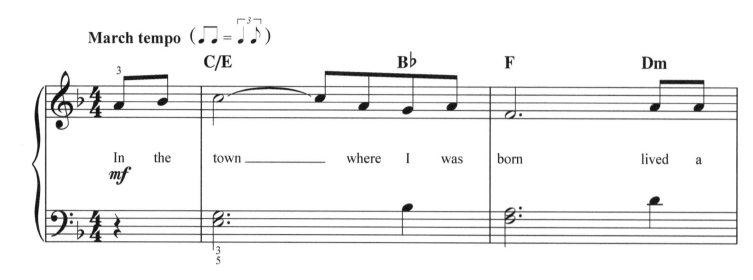

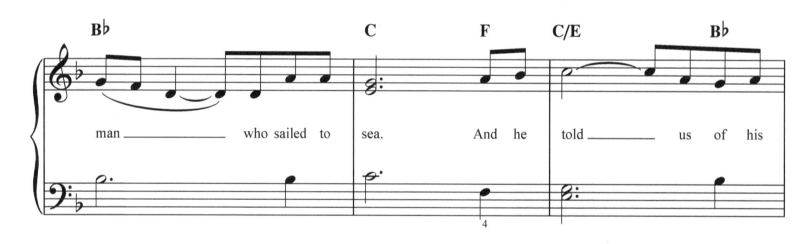

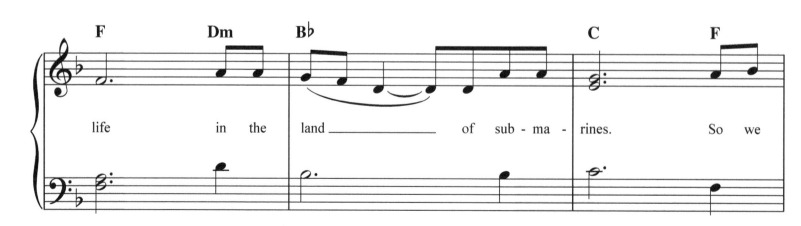

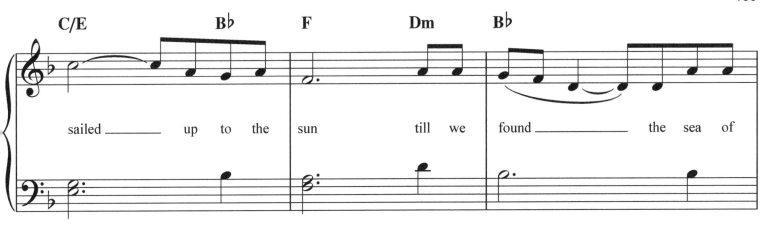

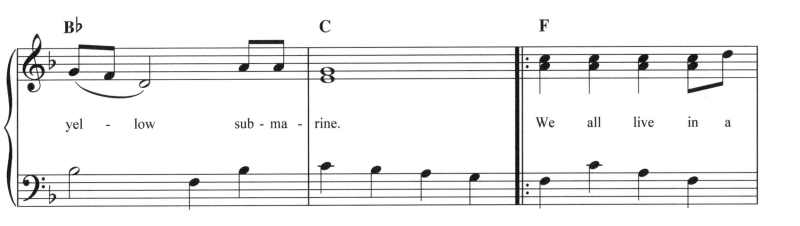

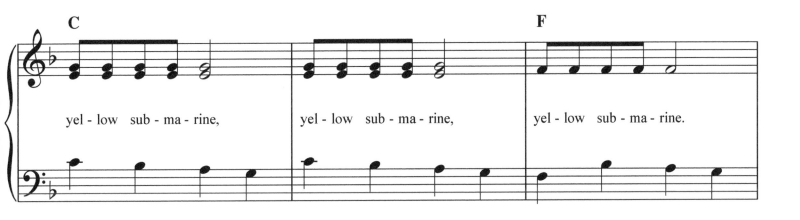

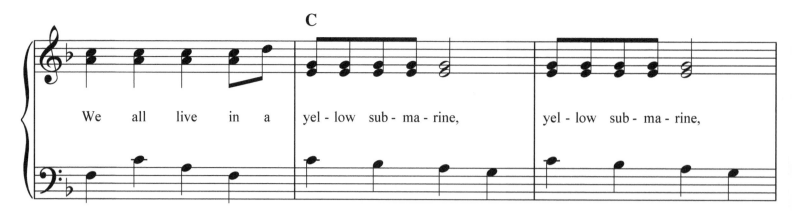

We all live in a yel - low sub - ma - rine, yel - low sub - ma - rine,

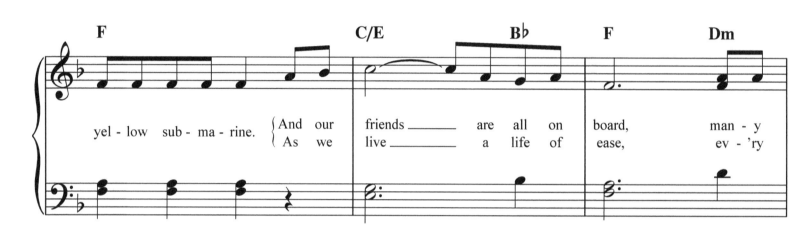

yel - low sub - ma - rine. { And our friends _____ are all on board, man - y
{ As we live _____ a life of ease, ev - 'ry

more of them _____ live next door. And the band _____ be - gins to
one of us _____ has all we need. Sky of blue _____ and sea of

1.

play:

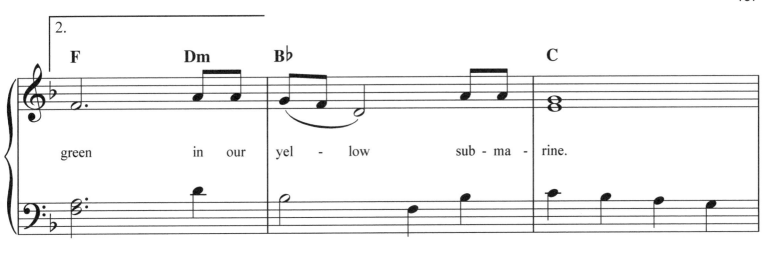

F   **Dm**   **B♭**   **C**

green   in our   yel - low   sub - ma - rine.

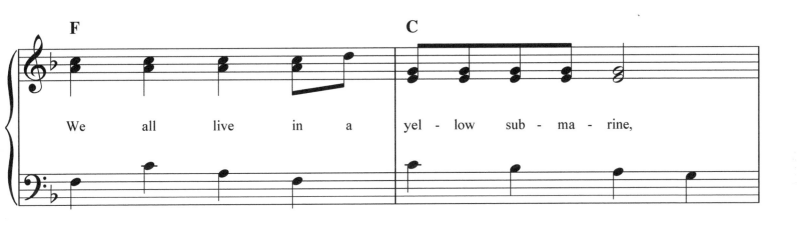

F   **C**

We   all   live   in   a   yel - low   sub - ma - rine,

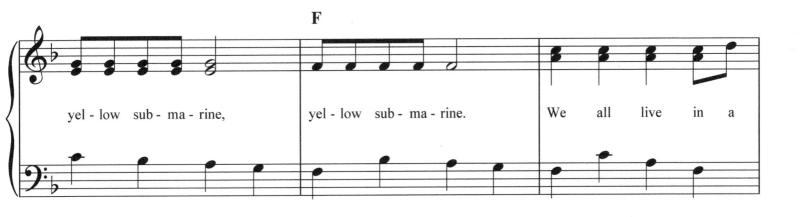

                   F

yel - low sub - ma - rine,   yel - low sub - ma - rine.   We   all   live   in   a

C   **F**

yel - low sub - ma - rine,   yel - low sub - ma - rine,   yel - low sub - ma - rine.

YOU'RE MY BEST FRIEND

Words and Music by
JOHN DEACON

Ooh, you make me live _____ what-
Ooh, you make me live _____ when-

ev - er this world can give to me. _____ It's you, you're all I _____ see. _____
ev - er this world is cruel to me. _____ I got you to help me for - give. _____

Ooh, you make me live _____ now, hon - ey,
Ooh, you make me live _____ now, hon - ey,

ooh, you make me live. ___ Oh, ___ you're the best ___
ooh, you make me live. ___ Oh, ___ you're the first ___

___ friend that I ___ ev - er had. ___ I've been with you such a long ___
___ one when things ___ turn out bad. ___ You know I'll nev - er be lone -

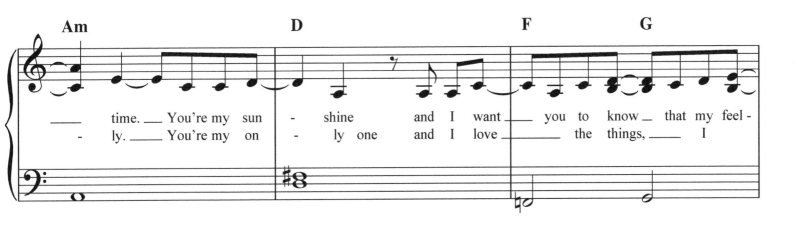

___ time. ___ You're my sun - shine and I want ___ you to know ___ that my feel -
- ly. ___ You're my on - ly one and I love ___ the things, ___ I

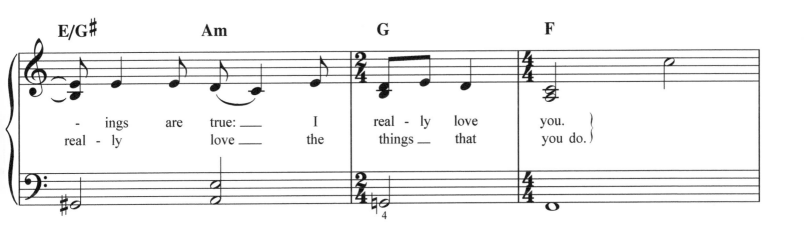

- ings are true: ___ I real - ly love you.
real - ly love ___ the things ___ that you do.

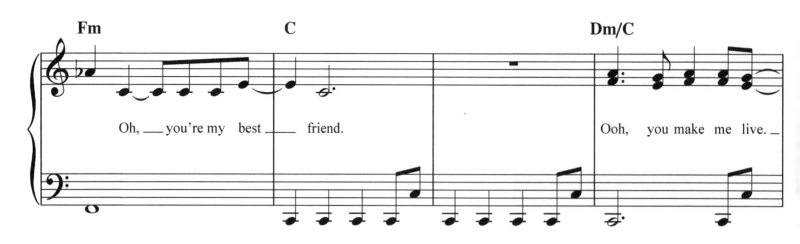

Oh, ___ you're my best ___ friend. Ooh, you make me live. ___

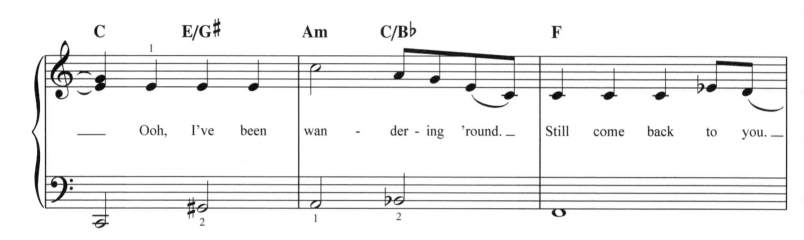

___ Ooh, I've been wan - der - ing 'round. ___ Still come back to you. ___

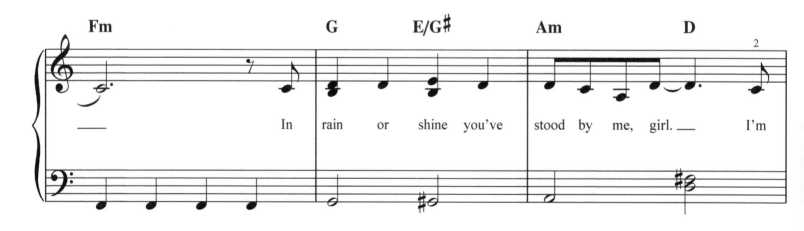

___ In rain or shine you've stood by me, girl. ___ I'm

hap - py at home, ___ you're my best ___ friend. ___

YOU'RE THE ONE THAT I WANT

from GREASE

Words and Music by
JOHN FARRAR

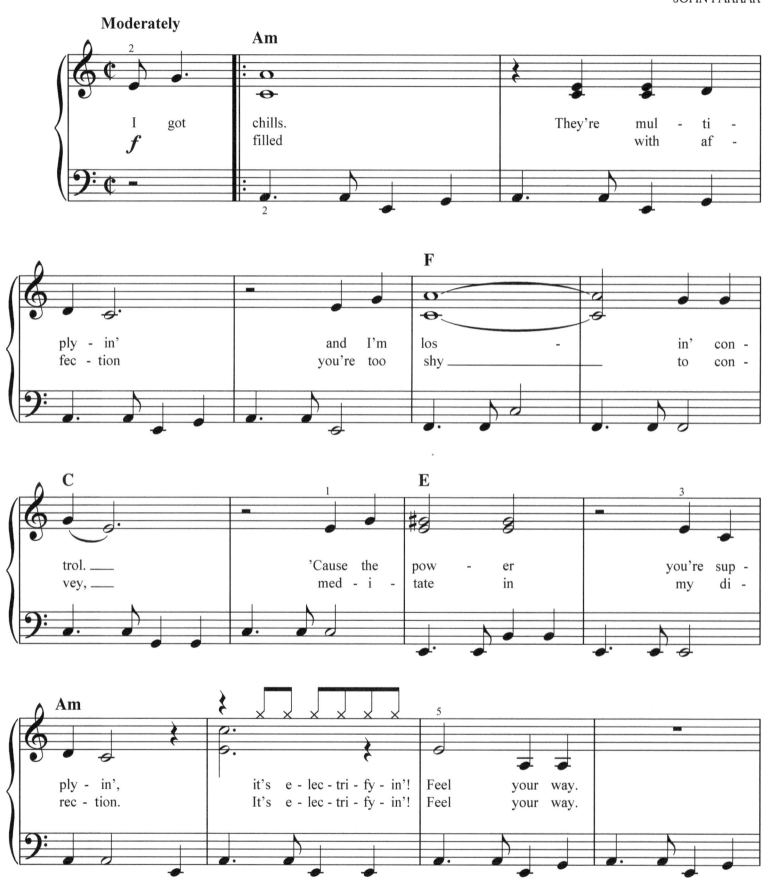

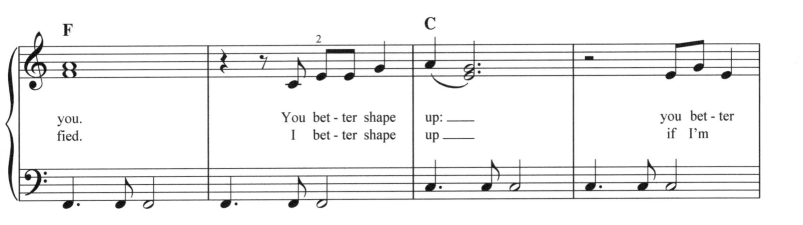

YOU'VE GOT A FRIEND

Words and Music by
CAROLE KING

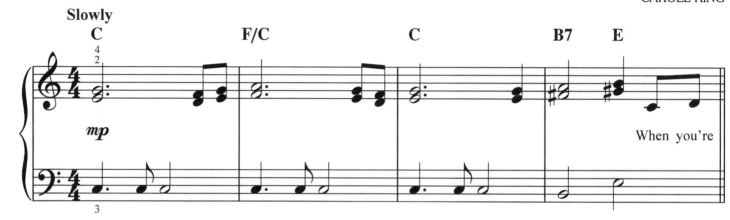

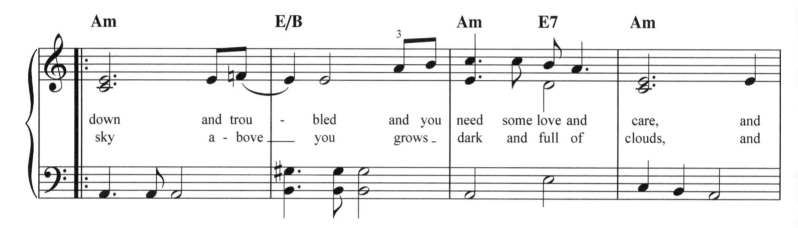

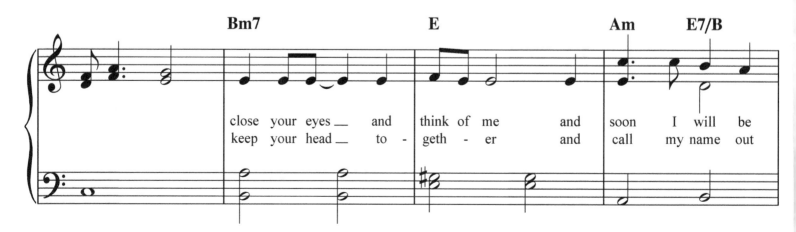

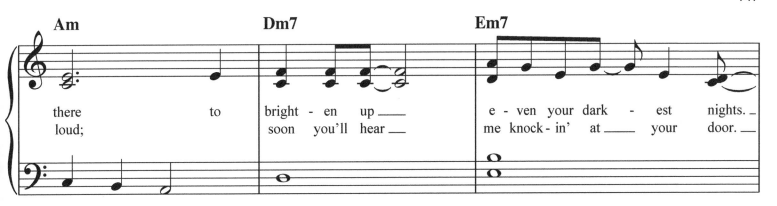

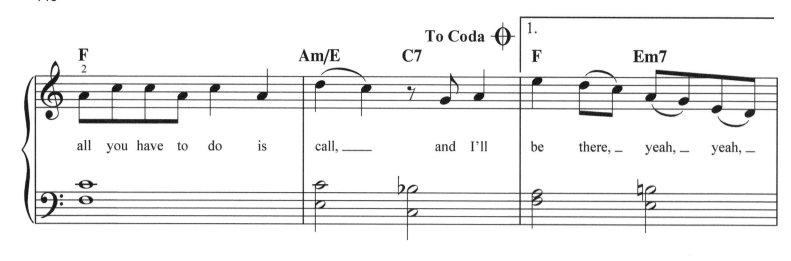

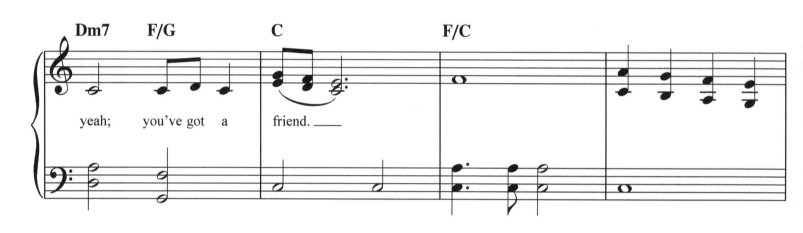

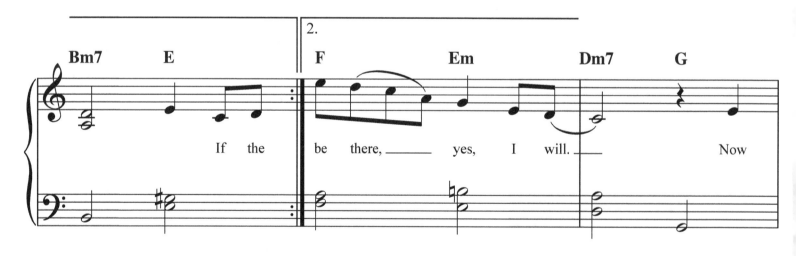

They'll hurt you, and de-sert you; they'll take your soul if you let

them. Oh, but don't you let them. You just

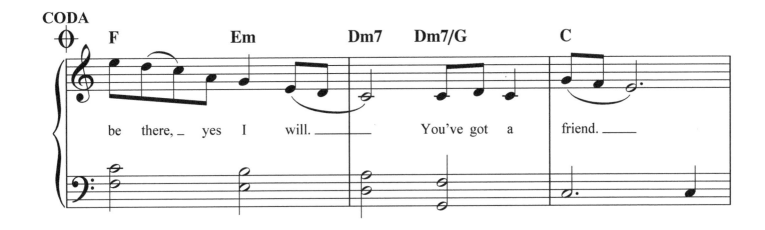

be there, yes I will. You've got a friend.

You've got a friend. Ain't it good to know you've got a friend.

WE ARE THE DINOSAURS

Words and Music by
LAURIE BERKNER

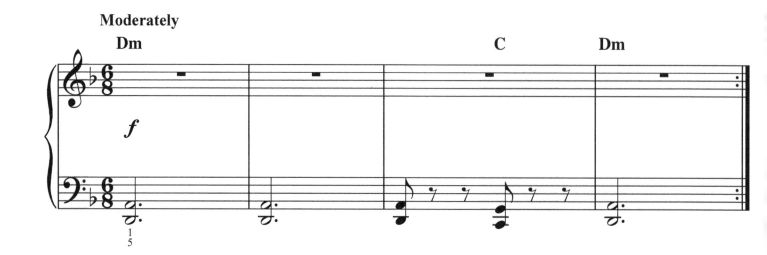

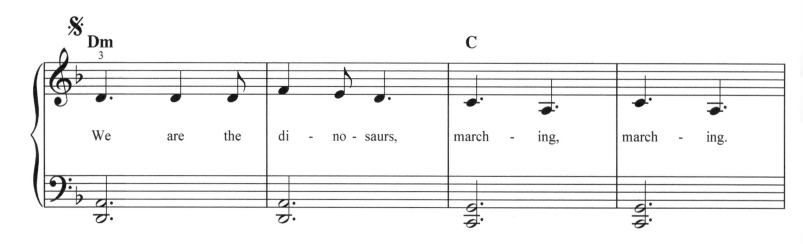

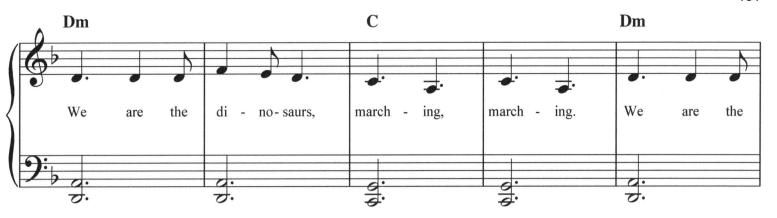

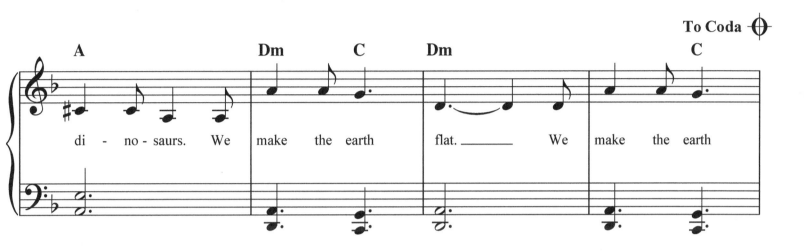

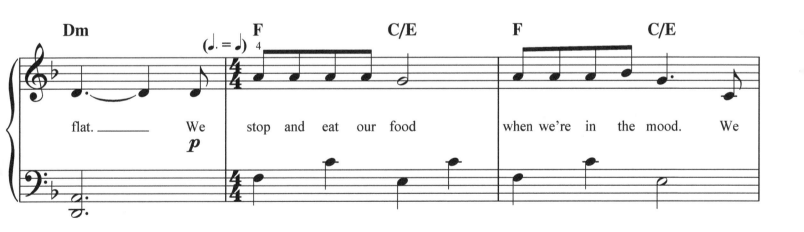

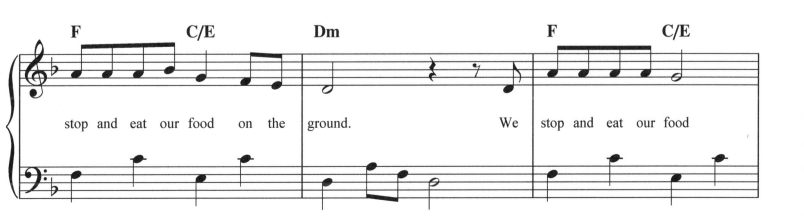

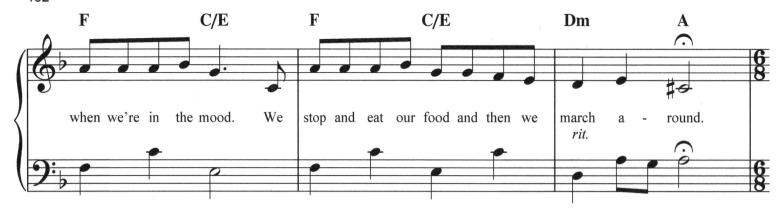

when we're in the mood. We stop and eat our food and then we march a - round.
rit.

D.S. al Coda

f a tempo

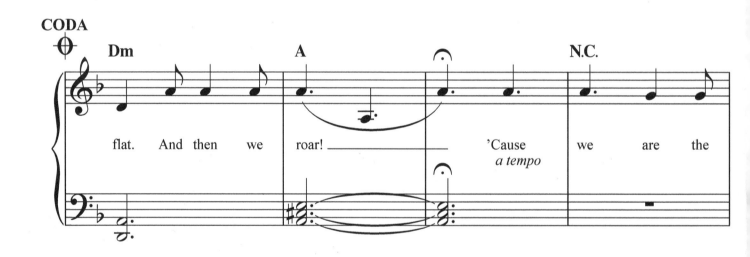

CODA

flat. And then we roar! 'Cause we are the
a tempo

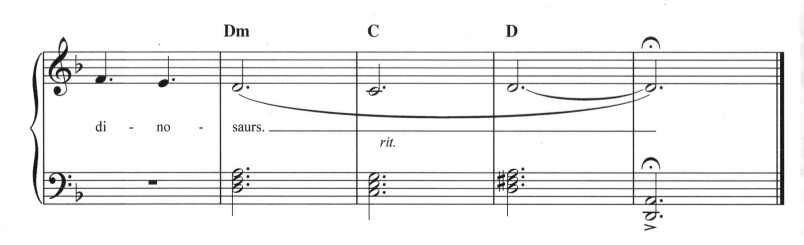

di - no - saurs.
rit.